Finding Frances...

LOVE LETTERS FROM A FLIGHT LIEUTENANT

At the age of 17, Eric Hutchin enlisted in the Royal Air Force. To learn to fly he was sent to Falcon Field, a private training base built in the city of Mesa in the Arizona desert and financed by Hollywood celebrities. There, while the Nazis established air superiority over most of Europe, Eric and his fellow cadets discovered Coca-Cola, rode horses cowboy-style, and learned to lay their lives on the line. Eric had a camera and he recorded it all. And he fell in love with Frances McKenzie, a beautiful 17-year-old American.

Throughout the war Eric wrote to Frances, filling hundreds of pages with his reflections, sketches, playful asides to the censors, and dreams of a different world. Though he couldn't say exactly what he was doing, Flight Lieutenant Hutchin was flying fighters. When Hitler bombarded England with V-1 rockets, Eric and his squadron would fly their Spitfires out over the English Channel and, with daring and precision, use the wingtips of their own aircraft to tilt the rockets and topple their gyros, deflecting them from their targets in the heart of England. Then he'd land and write to Frances.

She kept Eric's letters. Half a century after the armistice she gave them to his niece, Catherine Hutchin Harris, who lives not far from Falcon Field. Using recovered documents as well as Eric's love letters and original photos, she set out to tell his story. Clever and poignant, this is the personal chronicle of one flight lieutenant and his love for his special girl, but of course it's also the universal story — the true story — of every young man who goes to war.

Finding Frances...

LOVE LETTERS FROM A FLIGHT LIEUTENANT

CATHERINE HARRIS

Outskirts Press, Inc.
http://www.outskirtspress.com

ISBN: 978-1-4787-1717-1

Outskirts Press and the "OP" logo are trademarks belonging to Outskirts Press, Inc.

PRINTED IN THE UNITED STATES OF AMERICA

PER ARDUA AD ASTRA
The motto of the Royal Air Force
"Through Struggles to the Stars"

*This book is dedicated to all the wonderful young men of the Royal Air Force
whose courage and daring kept the Nazis from the shores of England.
We will never forget you.*

*It is also dedicated to my grandparents, Percival and Frances Hutchin,
and to my mother and father, Ernest and Deborah Hutchin,
who along with thousands of other Londoners survived night after night
of bombing, not knowing if they would be alive in the morning.
Your courage and resilience, along with your sense of humour,
has been a life lesson for our entire family.*

Royal Air Force badge reproduced with permission of the Ministry of Defence

The authoritative translation of the Royal Air Force motto is unsure, since there can be
a number of different meanings to "Ardua" and "Astra" and scholars have declared it
untranslatable. To the Royal Air Force and Commonwealth Air Forces, though,
it will remain "Through Struggles to the Stars".

ACKNOWLEDGMENTS

When I started this book I had no idea of the journey I would be taking. I have learned so much and will be forever thankful to the many people who contributed their knowledge and expertise. Inspiration came at first from the beautiful letters Eric wrote to Frances; I felt compelled to keep their love story alive and will always be grateful to Frances for keeping those letters.

Several books have been written about Falcon Field, including *Falcon Field: Life at Arizona's Falcon Field During WWII*, by Larry Simmons, *The RAF in Arizona: Falcon Field 1941 – 1945*, by Jim Dawson, and *Images of America – Falcon Field*, by Daryl F. Mallett. Each of these authors was motivational and liberal with his time, especially Daryl Mallett, who contacted me for input when he was writing his book and returned the favour when I was writing mine. In a work like this that melds iconic historical events, arcane technological detail and individual personal recollections from decades ago, there is no better fact-checking resource or photographic archive than Wikipedia.

Thanks go out to my dear friend Ken Beeby, a flight instructor at Falcon Field during the war, for his research and encouragement; Ken's colourful recollections of those days never cease to entertain and enlighten me. Very special thanks to Dr. P.E. van Loo, who edited *We Flew the Rocket Firing Typhoon*, published by the Royal Netherlands Air Force History Unit. Dr. Loo, your generosity with both your time and information has been invaluable to me. Rex Griswold's unfailing dedication to the history of Falcon Field has been an inspiration. Molly Turner generously shared her photographs and memories. Significant information was provided by Wing Leader Larry A. Turner of the Commemorative Air Force, Arizona Wing, Aviation Museum; Dr. John Rickard at *historyofwar.org*; Andrew Simpson, curator of the Department of Aircraft and Exhibitors at the Royal Air Force Museum in Hendon, England; and to the Air Historical Branch (RAF) Ministry of Defence. I also appreciate the assistance of Dee Ann Thomas and Corinne Nystrom, Falcon Field Airport, City of Mesa, and Rebecca Allen of the Mesa Public Library. Thanks to David Zaha at FedEx Office in Tucson for great customer service and to Tom Weinburg at Quik Print, always helpful over the years, who introduced me to Kate Erdmann, graphic designer extraordinaire.

Special thanks to friends and family: my brother and sister, Elizabeth and Paul Hutchin, for sharing their memories and photographs; my sister Carol for bringing me innumerable cups of tea; my great-niece Christiana for her computer help; my niece Katie for scanning all the photos; my nephew Sean for climbing into the attic and taking photographs of Eric's memorabilia; and to my friends in Hamburg, Ulli Paasch and Peter Zeiger for their love and kindness. I also deeply appreciate the contribution of a dear family friend, Jim Creasy, who continues to document our family history. Also thanks to Paul Stapleton-Smith for believing in me, to Ron Smithson for sharing his memories at Falcon Field and for his bravery as a bomber pilot in World War II, to Debbie Arthur for ongoing help, to Helen Garfinkle for proofreading and to Greg Landers, retired U.S. Navy captain and aviator, for input on the SS *Batory*. I am especially grateful to my close friend and neighbor, Judith Anderson, whose editorial expertise helped craft my manuscript into such a deeply personal tribute to my uncle.

Last but not least, thank you to my dear husband, Greg, for 25 special years of marriage, and for putting up with my endless hours at my desk when we could have been spending time together.

Finding Frances...

LOVE LETTERS FROM A FLIGHT LIEUTENANT

TABLE OF CONTENTS

CHAPTER ONE

Beginnings

This is the true story of Eric Hutchin, a young Royal Air Force fighter pilot who trained at Falcon Field, Mesa, Arizona, during World War II. There he fell in love with a 17-year-old American girl, Frances McKenzie. But let me start at the beginning.

Eric Geoffrey Hutchin was born in England on October 4th 1923 in High Garret, Essex, a small village about 25 miles northeast of London. Eric lived in Peartree Cottage with his mother, Frances, his father, Percival, and his two older brothers Frederick and Ernest. The boys attended Bocking Church Street School in Bocking, just outside Braintree, Essex.

Peartree Cottage. *Photograph by Elizabeth Hutchin*

TOP LEFT: The three brothers at scout camp.

TOP RIGHT: Swimming in the lake.

MIDDLE: Eric and Percy at Peartree Cottage.

RIGHT: Eric on left and Ernie.

Photographs from the Hutchin family archives.

They lived an enchanted life, helping out at a farm next door to the cottage. After the shire horses had toiled in the fields all day Eric and his brothers would collect them and ride them back to the farm, stopping at a pond where they would slake their thirst, and then the boys would continue their journey to the farm where they would help to stable the horses for the night. These times were among the fondest childhood memories of the Hutchin boys. They also thoroughly enjoyed riding their bicycles for miles and miles; their favourite pastime was to stop at the train station to watch the steam trains thundering through the countryside.

Their father, known as Percy, worked as a chauffeur for the Courtaulds, a wealthy local family, and Frances worked for them too. When Percy and Frances were away working for the Courtaulds the boys would stay with their paternal grandparents, Emily and Tom, to whom the brothers were very attached.

Gosfield Hall, Essex, family home of the Courtaulds.
Picture courtesy Steve Bartrick • www.antiqueprints.com

Samuel Courtauld (1846-1947), an English industrialist and founder of the Courtauld Institute of Art in London, was the great-nephew of textile magnate Samuel Courtauld Senior, who by 1809 had his own silk mill in Braintree. By the early 20th century the Courtauld family business had become a major international company, having successfully developed and marketed rayon, an artificial fibre and inexpensive silk substitute.

Most of the time Percy was chauffeur to Samuel's cousin Rene who was on the board of directors of Courtaulds, and when Rene moved to London in 1936 the Hutchin family moved to Wimbledon in South London.

Courtaulds Mill as it looked in the 1850s. The old mill built in 1809 is on the left.
Source Wikipedia

The mill as it looks today. It now houses a restaurant and an antique center.
Source Wikipedia

Eric attended Raynes Park County Grammar School for Boys, one of the leading schools in the area, where, under the tutelage of Mr. Claude Rogers, Eric's special aptitude for art and technical drawing was allowed to flourish. Upon graduating in 1939 at the age of 16 Eric was employed as a draughtsman for an electrical and mechanical company in Mitcham, Surrey, just outside London, where he remained until he decided to enroll in the Royal Air Force Volunteer Reserves. This decision was met with some resistance by his employer as Eric's expertise would be much needed in the years to come, but the nation's need for pilots was equally as pressing.

Meanwhile Percy was still driving for the Courtaulds and Frances was working at Foxboro Yoxall, a local factory. They loved to dance and spent their spare time going to many a dinner and dance at the Dog and Fox, a lovely hotel on Wimbledon Hill which still exists to this day.

Eric's two older brothers were also working. Ernie was 14 when he started working in a woodshop as a carpenter's mate, a job he did not like, and Fred (who was four years older than Ernie) had joined the Royal Air Force and was stationed in Canada. Eric and Ernie were very close, spending as much time together as they could when they were not at work. Eventually Ernie left his job at the woodshop and went to work

Ernest, Fredrick and Eric Hutchin (Brothers in Arms)

at Shannon Systems, where he met Deborah Kavanagh, the beautiful Irish woman he was to marry. In December of 1940 Ernie was called up for National Service and chose the Royal Air Force. He spent the next few months in training and doing his fair share of what he referred to as "square bashing."

In May of 1942 Ernie was posted to Hope Cove in Devonshire, a place he would return to as often as possible in the years to come. He applied for a position as an aircraft electrician, a job he loved. It seems that flying and aircraft are in the Hutchin family blood. In August of 1942 Ernie and Deborah were married in Carlton, Nottinghamshire, where Deborah was now living having been evacuated from London. After the wedding Ernie was posted to R.A.F. Station Wigsley, a mere 30 miles from Carlton. "What luck," Ernie said. Ernie worked on Stirling Bombers and then on Lancasters.

In November of 1943 Ernie's first child, Catherine, was born at City Hospital in Carlton (a mention of which is in one of Eric's letters), and although the bombings were not as bad in the northern part of England, Catherine came into the world on a foggy night during an air raid. Around this time Ernie's service in the Royal Air Force came to an end, and much to his disgust, he was transferred into the army. He was initially stationed in Aldershot and then posted to a Royal Engineers unit in Wales "miles from everything." He was then sent to Halifax in Yorkshire where he worked in an office and due to the fact that Deborah was expecting their second child he was granted a lot of leave. Carol was born on December 24th 1945 in Surrey and by this time Deborah was back in London and living with Ernie's parents.

In July 1946 Ernie was demobbed (an English expression from the word "demobilised") and was happy to return to his old job at Shannon's. By now Deborah was expecting their third child and Ernie and Deborah, who had been on a housing list for some time, were happy to move into a brand new council house. They moved there in October 1947. (The family still live there having purchased the house from the council several years ago.) Eric Geoffrey (who was named after his uncle) was born in July 1947 in Guildford, Surrey, all London hospitals being full at the time due to many "war babies" being born!

Ernest Hutchin

Ernie and Deborah were to have seven children together. After Catherine, Carol and Eric they had Paul, Elizabeth, Deborah and David. Ernie worked hard supporting his family, primarily as an electrician, and his last job before retirement was at Decca Navigator working on a cutting-edge navigational system for aeroplanes and flying on test flights of an Elizabethan, a 47-passenger, 5-crew plane.

Prior to this Eric's mother and father and brothers had lived through the dark years of World War II. The Hutchins, like most English families of the period, would bear the imprint of World War II for generations to come.

CHAPTER TWO

World War II and the Birth of Falcon Field

By autumn 1940 Britain had been at war for a year. Winston Churchill had replaced Neville Chamberlain as prime minister in May, just before a massive German offensive forced the evacuation of the British Expeditionary Force from Dunkirk. Germany had occupied the Channel Islands, just off the coast of Southern England. Throughout the summer and into the fall, the Royal Air Force valiantly defended England from the German Luftwaffe in the Battle of Britain, the first major campaign to be fought entirely in the air. The R.A.F. prevailed, but the cost in aircraft and pilots was staggering, inspiring Churchill's moving speech to the House of Commons on August 8, 1940:

> The gratitude of every home in our Island, in our Empire, and indeed throughout the world, except in the abodes of the guilty, goes out to the British airmen who, undaunted by odds, unwearied in their constant challenge and mortal danger, are turning the tide of the World War by their prowess and by their devotion. Never in the field of human conflict was so much owed by so many to so few. All hearts go out to the fighter pilots, whose brilliant actions we see with our own eyes day after day; but we must never forget that all the time, night after night, month after month, our bomber squadrons travel far into Germany, find their targets in the darkness by the highest navigational skill, aim their attacks, often under the heaviest fire, often with serious loss, with deliberate careful discrimination, and inflict shat-

tering blows upon the whole of the technical and war-making structure of the Nazi power.

The massive bombing of the London Blitz began the same month. Britain was facing a critical shortage of pilots to combat these raids over England, and Churchill and his staff recognized that their main challenge lay in trying to train inexperienced fliers in crowded skies, in bad weather, in the middle of a war. At this time America was neutral and Congress was embroiled in debate over isolationist policy, but President Roosevelt and many military leaders realized the United States would eventually be drawn into the war. It was not prepared. The U.S. Army Air Corps had a single flying school, at Randolph Field in San Antonio, Texas. It could train only 500 pilots a year.

General Henry Harley "Hap" Arnold, acting Deputy Chief of Staff of the Army as well as Chief of the Air Corps, was a firm supporter of military aid to Britain. By the end of 1940 he was looking for ways to increase and accelerate flight training for U.S. airmen and help Britain do the same while the United States officially maintained a policy of non-intervention. General Arnold started contacting private flying school operators to talk about creating civilian training schools for military fighter pilots. In his vision, the civilian operator, under contract to the Air Corps, would provide the instructors, maintenance crew, logistical staff, food and housing, while the Air Corps would supply the aircraft and the cadets. He figured they could train about 2,400 pilots a year.

In March 1941 The Lend-Lease Act was approved in Congress. It authorised a commitment to a program that would train 4,000 British pilots. Formally titled "An Act to Further Promote the Defense of the United States," it allowed America to supply material to the United Kingdom, the Soviet Union, China, Free France, and other Allied nations, essentially ending any pretence of neutrality. Under this program, six British Flying Training Schools (BFTS) were set up in the United States in the summer of 1941:

1. BFTS Terrell, Texas   4. BFTS Mesa, Arizona
2. BFTS Lancaster, California   5. BFTS Clewiston, Florida
3. BFTS Miami, Oklahoma   6. BFTS Ponca City, Oklahoma

A seventh, 7 BFTS at Sweetwater, Texas, opened in May 1942 but closed in August. By 1945 110,000 airmen were trained by such contract schools.

General Arnold was present in August 1941 when Winston Churchill and President Roosevelt met on the USS *Augusta* to develop the Atlantic Charter. While they defined the goals of the Allies and established a vision for a post–World War II world, General Arnold helped broker an agreement that provided for Army Air Force aircraft to be used for British Flying Training Schools under the terms of Lend-Lease. By September Arnold's staff had produced a plan to allot 66 percent of all American tactical aircraft production to Lend-Lease, with half of those aircraft going to Britain and the Commonwealth.

Winston Churchill and Franklin D. Roosevelt on board
the USS *Augusta*, August 1941.

Photograph courtesy
Franklin D. Roosevelt Presidential Library and Museum, New York

During the time Eric Hutchin was enduring basic training as a Royal Air Force cadet in England, two American businessmen, John (Jack) Connelly and Leland Hayward, a prominent Hollywood producer, saw an investment opportunity. As soon as Congress authorised the contract flying schools, they decided to become involved in military pilot training. Both men had an aviation background. Connelly was a Civil Aviation authority and Hayward was a pilot, having been trained in the U.S. Navy during World War I. They enlisted John Swope, a commercial pilot and photographer, to oversee the training of aviation cadets. Together they formed Southwest Airways, finding much of their start-up funding in Hollywood through such prominent figures as James Stewart, Henry Fonda, Cary Grant, Ginger Rogers, Hoagy Carmichael and Daryl F. Zanuck.

In March 1941 Southwest Airways opened Thunderbird Field near Glendale, Arizona. They soon expanded their training enterprise with two other Arizona airfields, Falcon Field at Mesa (operational in September 1941) and Thunderbird Field #2 in Scottsdale (June 1942). Jack Connelly had wanted all the Southwest training fields to be called "Thunderbird," but the British apparently demurred. According to one popular story, Connelly was told the falcon had been an English noble bird of prey since Norman times, and the British wanted their base to be called Falcon Field. "That [the thunderbird] may be your bird," they said, "but this is our field and our bird is the falcon."

By the end of the war, Southwest Airways was the largest contract company in the nation, having trained over 20,000 pilots from two dozen countries. In 1958 it changed its name to Pacific Air Lines and in 1968 merged with other lines to become Air West. The present-day carrier Southwest Airlines is a completely unrelated company established in 1967.

Falcon Field September 1941
The roof is on the east hanger and a concrete slab has been poured for
the west hanger. The four L-shaped buildings are the barracks.

At Falcon the cadets' entire training course was 29 weeks long and was conducted at a single field, unlike the standard American programme, which conducted three consecutive stages at different bases. Arizona weather was perfect for training the cadets. Falcon took pride in a record of 400 days of uninterrupted flying, with fewer than 10 days lost to bad weather over a period of four years. According to a maintenance chief, Falcon crews did their jobs for a third of the cost the government had estimated and were well below the expected fatality rate. At one time 60 percent of the mechanics were women.

There was an additional Hollywood connection at Falcon. The Field and many of the cadets were featured in *Thunder Birds: Soldiers of the Air* (1942), a 20th Century–Fox movie starring Gene Tierney. It was one of a number of propaganda films intended to promote support for the war and the international training program. (One alternative title was *A Tommy in the USA*.) The studio built a swimming pool for use in the movie and as a thank-you they gifted it to Falcon for the young soldiers

Falcon Field in full operation at the end of 1941
*Photographs of Falcon Field courtesy Commemorative Air Force,
Arizona Wing, Aviation Museum*

of the air heading off to the real war.

All U.S. Army Air Force graduates from flight school were officers, because all pilots in the Air Force were commissioned. All the R.A.F. graduates, on the other hand, were sergeants, even though they passed the same course. The better trainees were often offered a guaranteed commission if they would stay in the United States or Canada as instructors, but the vast majority wanted to go home to fight for England.

In all, 23 British cadets, one American cadet and four instructors were killed in training at Falcon Field and are now buried in the Mesa City Cemetery, along with several of their colleagues who have since died of natural causes. Several thousand pilots were trained there before the R.A.F. installation was closed at the end of World War II. The City of Mesa purchased the field from the U.S. government for $1 and it still remains an active airfield to this day.

The British cadets who trained in the United States were often treated like sons or brothers by the Americans, and there are numerous websites dedicated to the memory of that powerful relationship. The lines below, written in 1942 by a pilot who had completed his training at 5 BFTS Riddle Field, in Clewiston, Florida, were found at *www.ww2aircraft.net*:

EPILOGUE
Wherere the British flag is flown
With the Stars and Stripes above
You'll find a kindred unity
of friendship and of love;
Each British heart beneath those flags —
Whoever it may be —
Says "Thank you" to America,
"For what you've been to me."

CHAPTER THREE

A Transatlantic Journey

The dark clouds of World War II had shadowed Europe for 17 months when Eric, who had always dreamed of flying and had been in the R.A.F. Volunteer Reserves since 1939, was accepted into service in February 1941 as an Aircraftman Second Class with the added description Pilot Under Training/Observer. Initial training, as a Royal Air Force Cadet, commenced at Durham University Air School. This was followed by a short stay at Lord's Cricket Ground in London's St. John's Wood for tests and kitting out, and then he was off to R.A.F. Aberystwyth in West Wales followed by R.A.F. Ansty near Coventry and finally on to another temporary holding camp at Heaton Park in Manchester, where he learned that he would be going to America for flight training.

In May 1942 Eric Hutchin was among a large contingent of young R.A.F. cadets headed to the United States and Falcon Field for pilot training. They set sail on the MS *Batory* from Liverpool, England, on a 10 day hazardous convoy across the Atlantic to Halifax, Nova Scotia, Canada. The MS *Batory* was used to transport Allied troops throughout the war

MS *Batory. Source - Wikipedia*

and secretly transported much of Britain's gold reserves to Montreal, Canada, for safekeeping. The cadets travelled on the fast liner rather than a convoy ship, in an effort to avoid the U-boats patrolling the waters of the Atlantic. At Halifax the cadets went on to a holding camp at Moncton, New Brunswick, where they were assigned to the various airfields to be trained as fighter pilots. Eric drew Falcon Field, Mesa, Arizona. Training in England was not an option as the beautiful green countryside was under constant siege by the Nazis.

Picture courtesy Chuck Baker
www.brownie-camera.com

Eric was an avid photographer and had his Baby Brownie Special camera tucked under his arm as he travelled across America and documented his life at Falcon Field. (Unless otherwise noted all black-and-white photographs are Eric's.)

Quebec across the St. Lawrence River

Montreal

Postcard
from Montreal,
June 17, 1942

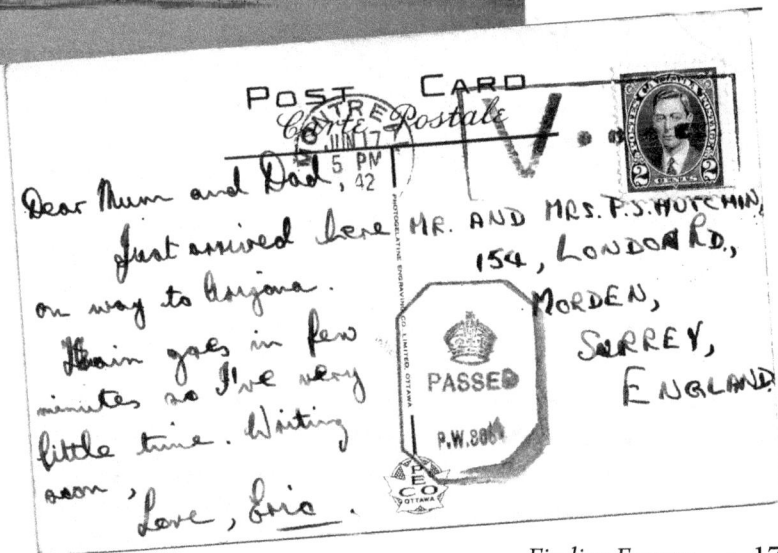

Dear Mum and Dad,
    Just arrived here
on way to Arizona.
Train goes in few
minutes so I've very
little time. Writing
soon, Love, Eric.

MR. AND MRS. P.S. HUTCHIN,
154, LONDON RD.,
MORDEN,
SURREY,
ENGLAND

Starting their difficult yet exciting train journey across America the cadets stopped in Chicago at La Salle Station, where Eric photographed one of the first diesel trains in America as well as the steam train in which the cadets were travelling.

ABOVE: Chicago La Salle Station, the Rock Island Express. This is the train Eric travelled on from Canada to Phoenix. Note the cadets posing on the front of the engine.

RIGHT: The Rock Island Diesel, La Salle Station.

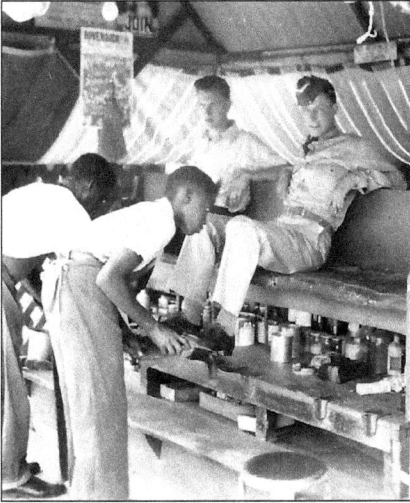

Eric getting a quick shoeshine
in Chicago

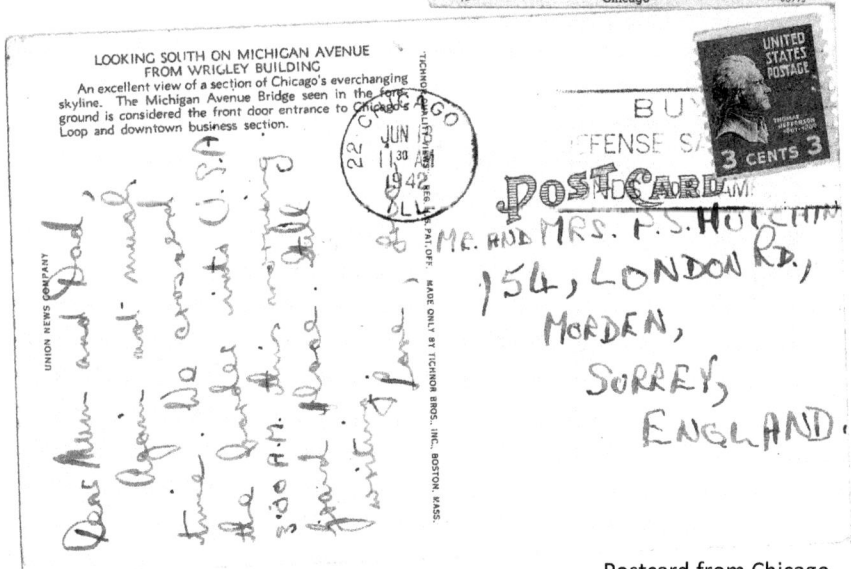

Postcard from Chicago,
June 18, 1942

The journey continues…

The Arsenal Bridge across the Mississippi River with the Rock Island Centennial
Bridge in the background. The bridge connects Rock Island, Illinois,
and Davenport, Iowa.

And on through Kansas…

Postcard from Kansas City,
June 18, 1942

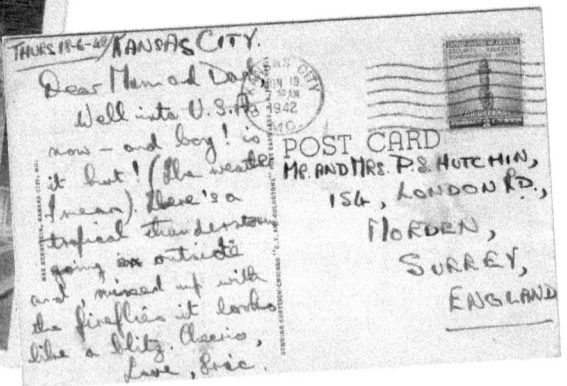

The Golden State Express, Tucumcari, New Mexico

Sonoran Desert, Douglas, Arizona

HELL IN ARIZONA
By the Author of "Arizona a Paradise"

The Devil in Hell we're told was chained,
And a thousand years he there remained,
He neither complained nor did he groan,
But determined to start a hell of his own.

Where he could torment the souls of men,
Without being chained in a prison pen.
So he asked the Lord if he had on hand
Anything left when he made this land.

The Lord said "Yes, I have plenty on hand,
But I left it down on the Arizona Sand.
The fact is 'old boy' the stuff is so poor
I don't think you can use it in hell any more."

But the Devil went down to look at the truck
And said if he took it as a gift he was stuck,
For after examining it carefully and well,
He concluded the place was too dry for a hell.

So in order to get it off His hand
The Lord promised the Devil to water the land.
For He had some water or rather some dregs,
A regular cathartic and smelled like bad eggs.

The heat in the summer is one hundred and ten,
Too hot for the Devil and too hot for men;
The wild boar roams through the black chaparral;
'Tis a hell of a place that he has for a hell.

Hence the trade was closed and the deed was given,
And the Lord went back to his home in heaven;
The Devil said to himself "I have all that is needed,
To make a good hell" and hence he succeeded.

He began to put thorns all over the trees,
And mixed up the sands with millions of fleas.
He scattered tarantulas along the roads;
Put thorns on cactus and horns on toads,

He lengthened the horns of the Desert steers,
And put an addition to the rabbits' ears;
He put a little devil in the broncho steed
And poisoned the feet of the centipede.

The rattlesnake bites you, the scorpion stings,
The mosquito delights you with his buzzing wings,
The sand-burs prevail and so do the ants
And those who sit down need half soles on their
    pants.

The Devil then said that throughout the land
He'd arrange to keep up the Devil's own brand,
And all should be Mavericks unless they bore,
Marks or scratches of bites and thorns by the score

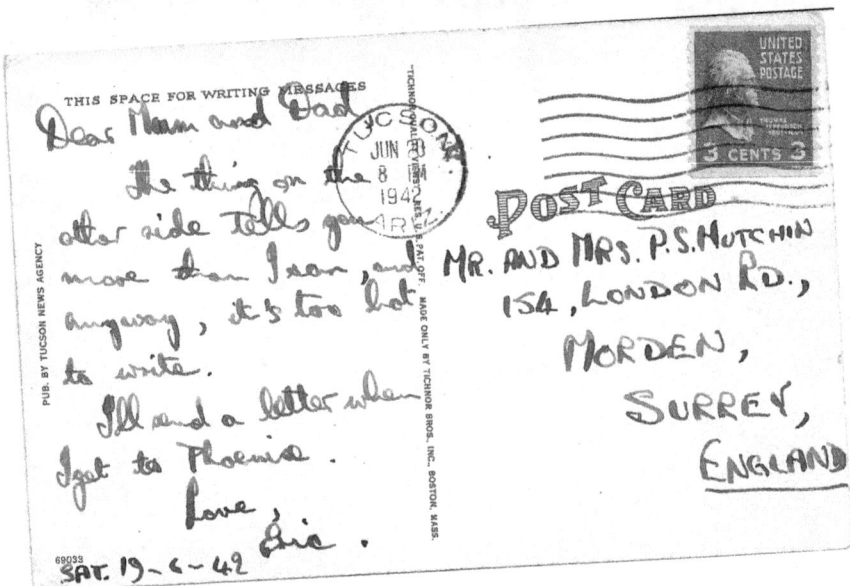

THIS SPACE FOR WRITING MESSAGES

Dear Mum and Dad

The thing on the other side tells you more than I can, and anyway, it's too hot to write.

I'll send a letter when I get to Phoenix.

Love,
Eric.

SAT. 19 – 6 – 42

MR. AND MRS. P.S. HUTCHIN
154, LONDON RD.,
MORDEN,
SURREY,
ENGLAND

Postcard from Tucson, Arizona, June 19, 1942
The last stop before arriving in Phoenix and Falcon Field, Mesa

CHAPTER FOUR
Life at Falcon Field, Course 10

In May 1942 Eric had been duly assigned to No.4 British Flying School at Falcon Field, Mesa, Arizona, having been promoted to Leading Aircraftman in January of that year. In June he was one of 54 cadets enrolled in Course 10.

The main building at Falcon Field
with its tower was a welcome sight for the road-weary cadets.
Photograph courtesy Molly Turner

Training commenced in earnest on June 23 on the Boeing-Stearman PT-13D a bi-plane similar to the British de Havilland Tiger Moth. Some of the airmen no doubt struggled to come to terms with a propeller that rotated in a reverse direction to that of the Tiger Moths they had previously been used to.

Boeing Stearman PT-13D.
Photograph courtesy Molly Turner

After the Stearman the cadets moved on to the more complex single engine monoplane, the Vultee BT-13A Valiant. Heavier and faster than the primary trainer, with a more powerful engine, the Valiant came to be known as the "Vultee Vibrator" due to its propensity to shake at various speeds. Training was rounded off on the North American AT-6A Texan with its 42-foot wingspan and length of 29 feet (four variants built for the British were called the Harvard). During this time the cadets also received intensive training in the classroom, learning navigation procedures, flight planning, communication, radio navigation, flying on instruments and much, much more.

Vultee BT-13 Valiant.
Photograph courtesy Molly Turner

Course 10. Eric in the middle row, 3rd from left.

At Falcon Field Eric struck up friendships with two people who were to mean a great deal to him. The first was Flying Officer Ian Briscoe, who hailed from Formby in Lancashire. Eric and Ian went on to become fast friends and flew together with 182 Squadron after leaving Falcon.

During this time a group named the British War Relief Society opened an old house within walking distance from downtown Phoenix. They furnished it with cots and a large tea table and invited a group of high school girls to come over to provide the boys with a means of meeting local people. Not long afterwards Eric met the second person who was to mean so much to him, the love of his life, the beautiful Frances McKenzie.

Eric and Ian,
Phoenix 1942

Frances

TOP: Friends on a trip to the Grand Canyon.

BOTTOM LEFT: Stormy weather at the base.

BOTTOM RIGHT: Eric was fascinated by the palm trees!

TOP LEFT: Relaxing at the pool (Eric in the middle).

TOP RIGHT: Eric posing.

BOTTOM: The swimming pool built by 20th Century–Fox.
Photograph courtesy Molly Turner

ABOVE: Joe Wischler was chief of maintenance at Falcon. Some of his crew, including the ladies pictured above, were responsible for washing the aircraft.
Photograph courtesy Molly Turner.

RIGHT: The Barracks.

ABOVE: Eric is the handsome one on the right.

LEFT MIDDLE: Eric's buddies discovering Coca-Cola!

LEFT BOTTOM: In the canteen drinking something other than Coca-Cola. Eric is at the far left with a glass of wine.

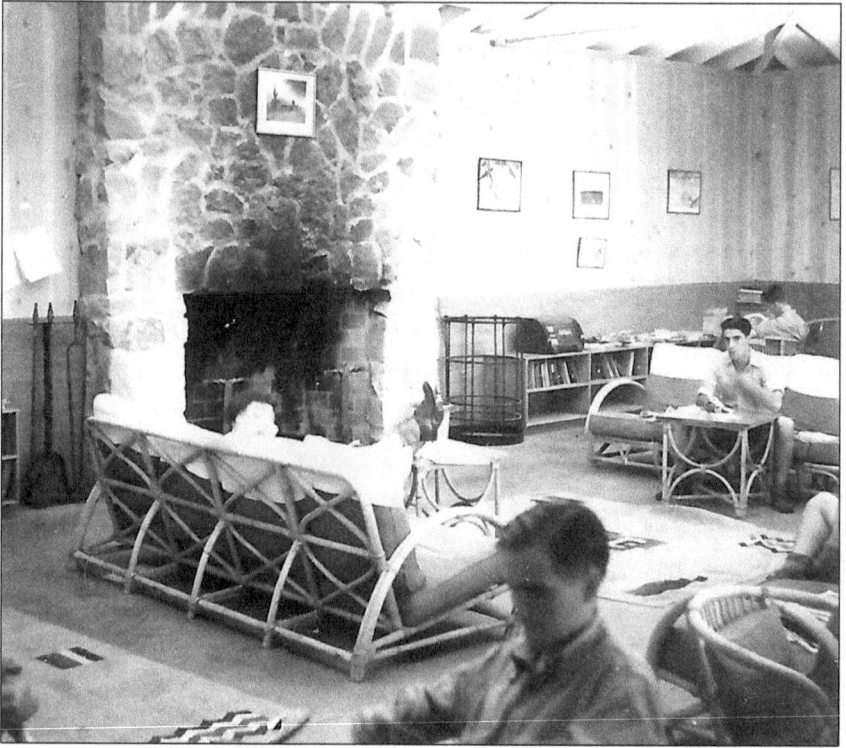
Sitting around the fireplace in the cadets' lounge.

Eric horseback riding in the Sonoran
Desert, Tucson, Arizona

In September 1942, during one of the breaks from training, Eric and some friends went to Los Angeles for some much-needed rest and relaxation. They had a fantastic time in Los Angeles and Hollywood tripping the light fantastic. One of the places where they danced the night away was the Earl Carroll Theatre-Restaurant in Hollywood.

801—Earl Carroll Theatre-Restaurant, Hollywood, California

The Earl Carroll Theatre-Restaurant in the heart of Hollywood on Sunset Boulevard near Vine, is a favorite Nite Spot in the Film Capital of the World. Seating arrangements are terraced so all guests may enjoy an-obstructed view of the lavish stage production with "Sixty of the Most Beautiful Girls in the World."

Dear Folks,
    This is where we went last night — 8 p.m. till 2·30 A.M. — what a night! I'll write when I get back — haven't time at the moment.
        S'long,
            Eric.

POST CARD

MR. AND MRS. P.S. HUTCHIN,
154, LONDON RD.,
MORDEN,
SURREY,
ENGLAND.

Postcard from Los Angeles,
Sept 21, 1942

TOP: At Florentine Gardens, Hollywood — Eric standing in back with his arm on Ian's shoulder. Unknown pretty lady.

BOTTOM: The folder in which Eric received the photograph.

It was during this visit to Los Angeles that Eric met the beautiful English film star Anna Neagle, who was under contract to RKO Radio Pictures. Miss Neagle was one of the most popular English film actresses of her time. She made many films, including *Irene* (1940) with Ray Milland, *No, No Nanette* (1940) with Victor Mature, *Sunny* (1941) with Ray Bolger, and her final film under contract with RKO, *Forever and a Day* (1943), again with Ray Milland. Eric and his pals had a great time with Miss Neagle, spending time with her at her hotel pool and later at the "Batory" nightclub and drinking beer at Lucey's (pictured below). Upon returning to Falcon Field Eric received the following letter from Miss Neagle who was obviously quite smitten with "the lads."

TOP LEFT: Lucey's Restaurant and nightclub, where Eric and his friends spent time with Anna Neagle.

ABOVE RIGHT: Candid photograph Eric took of Miss Neagle sans make-up!

LEFT: Sitting around the pool in Hollywood with Anna Neagle and friends.

RKO RADIO PICTURES, INC.

780 GOWER STREET, LOS ANGELES, CALIF.

REG. U.S. PAT. OFF.

September 24th,
1 9 4 2

Dear L.A.C. Hutchin:

      Here are the photographs I promised the
lads. I'm so sorry I do not know your Christian
name as I would like to have autographed your
picture a little more personally. I'm also sending
you the match cover from the "Batory", one from
Lucey's which is where we had beer last night, and
another one from The Players' Club which you may
have seen whilst in Hollywood.

      It was simply grand meeting you all, and
I hope so much that some day our paths may cross
again. Please give the boys my very best wishes
and the hope that everything may go well with you
all.

Sincerely,

Anna Neagle

1385447 L.A.C. Hutchin
10 Course,
Falconfield,
Mesa, Arizona

P.S. I'd love to have one or two of the snapshots
as a souvenir of yesterday, so could you send them
to me at the St. Regis Hotel, 55th Street and Fifth
Avenue, New York City? I leave here tomorrow.

ABOVE: Graduation ceremonies at Falcon Field. *Photograph courtesy Molly Turner.*

LEFT: Au Revoir. *Photograph courtesy Molly Turner.*

Course 10 ended on December 31, 1942, and the following day Eric received his Wings, the uniform insignia that identified him as a pilot, from Wing Commander John Fergus McKenna, A.F.C. Training over, the newly qualified graduates were given the opportunity to let their hair down with a party held at the Westward Ho Hotel in nearby Phoenix, and Eric enjoyed the evening enlivened by local young women, including Frances McKenzie, who had been especially invited to make things swing. By then Eric knew he was in love with Frances and had been invited by her parents to spend some time at their home during Christmas. Eric corresponded with Frances at length upon his return to England and wrote her the most beautiful letters throughout the war.

Westward Ho Hotel, Phoenix, where Eric danced with Frances
at his graduation from Falcon Field Course 10.

Of the 54 cadets who reported for training on Course 10 that June day, 12 passed out as pilot officers (Eric being one of them), 36 as flight sergeants, 5 were assigned other duties, and 1 was held over to Course 11. Sadly 21 on the course were destined not to survive through the war while another was killed in a May 1948 flying accident.

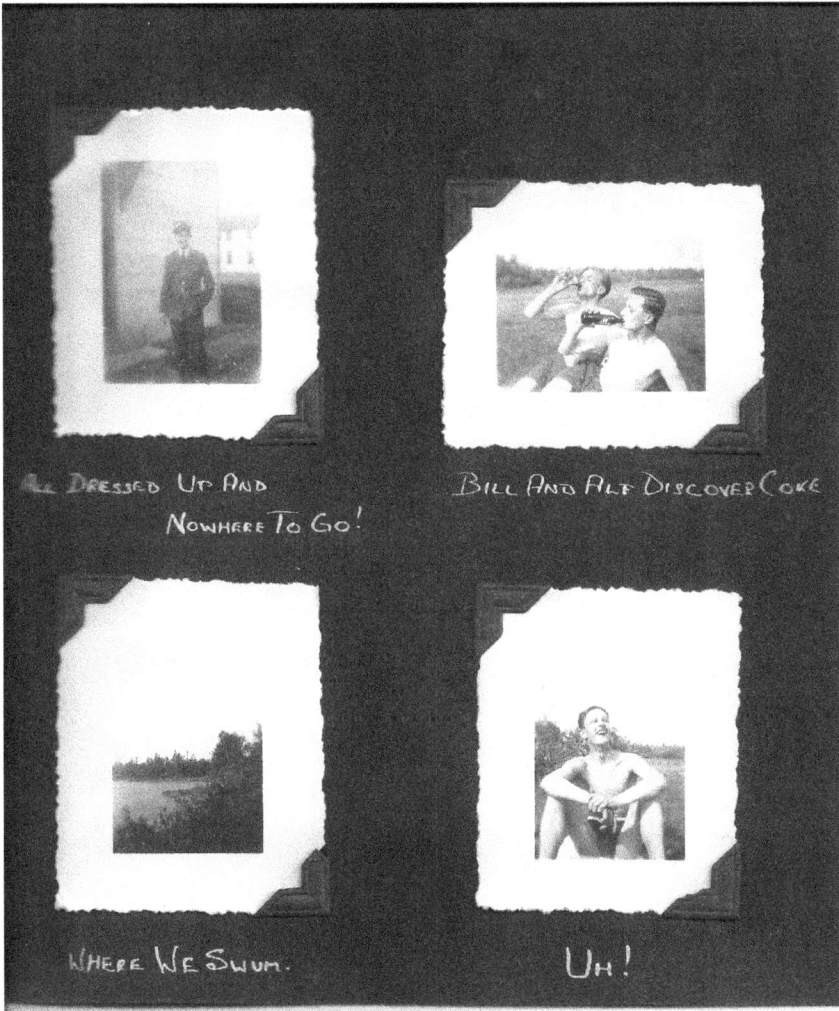

Pages from Eric's photo album where he fastidiously and humourously notated each picture.

More from Eric's photo album.

CHAPTER FIVE
Life After Falcon Field

Eric spent Christmas 1942 with Frances, having been invited to spend a couple of nights at her home with her parents. This was a Christmas he fondly remembered as one of the happiest times of his life. It was also the first time he kissed her. He left Arizona in January 1943 with a heavy heart, one that would forever belong to Frances. Back at Moncton he was promoted to Pilot Officer in the general duties branch of the Royal Air Force and following is the first of many letters he wrote to Frances:

Pilot Officer E. G. Hutchin
Transient Officers Mess,
R.A.F.Moncton, N.B., CANADA

January 8th, 1943

My Dear Frances,
I found this letter rather hard to start. Five sheets have already been torn up! You see I have such a lot to say. I don't know where to begin. But when I get going there'll be no stopping me. First I'll tell you about George. George is a black widow spider who slipped out of my shoe at Falcon one day. He seemed to see in me in a sort of kindred spirit! for he has since followed me around like Mary's lamb. Unfortunately he insists

on drinking far too much of any liquid he can lay his hands on, or whatever spiders have. And when I am writing letters he gets disgustingly tight on ink. Like most other animals, when he's tight he's uncontrollable and wanders around all over the paper. That is a rather complicated way of apologizing for my writing, which you'll admit looks as though an inebriated spider had crawled over the letter. Another thing I must apologize for is this notepaper, which is all I have on board at the moment. I've not been able to muster sufficient energy or cash to buy any more but I guess it'll get there just the same.

The train journey was a four day nightmare. Fifty of us were packed in one car and that wasn't a sleeper. However Ten Course did things to that car that had never been done before! We dismantled the seats and built them up again until they at least looked like beds, and by pushing a few fellows on to the floor we managed to make ourselves fairly comfortable. However, at around 2:00 am the heating system burst and flooded the car, much to the disgust of the chaps on the floor, so we shivered the rest of the night away until we reached Tucumcari in New Mexico and got a new car. However, that night we discovered the car had no lights, and we had to sit in darkness for about three hours. This was not without its amusing points however, for other passengers (civilians) were wandering through and from what I could hear the boys were enjoying themselves immensely. At Kansas City we were fitted up with lights again just in time to go to bed! On this station Ian was practically embraced by a large lady who thought "you boys are just too, too wonderful"! Snow began to appear as soon as we left Tucumcari and by the time we arrived in Chicago at 12:30 pm Monday afternoon the mercury had retired coyly into the bulb. At Chicago we missed our connection, so we spent the remainder of the day wandering around the city. The train left at 8:00 pm and we were joined on it by fellows from Lancaster.

Some time early on Tuesday morning, we crossed the border and made Montreal that night. Here we held the train up for two hours while we raided the station restaurant, and then spent our last night travelling — the most comfortable, even though it was a Canadian train! All day Wednesday, we did nothing but gaze on snow and ice, and at about 9:00 pm that night we arrived in Moncton. We crawled out of the train and nearly died of exposure on the spot! Boy, was it cold! The roads are merely sheets of ice about two inches thick. We had to stagger over two miles of them to the camp. Sliding around all over the place, and when we eventually arrived they weren't expecting us. However we found a place to rest our weary bones and by the next morning they had got organised. The commissions haven't come through yet, but we're expecting them any day now.

Meanwhile, they're still pushing us around as if we are cadets. The fellows are beginning to realize just how good it was at Falcon, and all I hear all day is "I wish

I was back in dear old Phoenix." I'm darn sure I do and not merely because of the climate either. This last page had to be completely rewritten, because I said on the original lots of things I shouldn't have and which no one in his right senses would have dreamed of writing. That I'm afraid is why this letter has taken such a darn long time to write. Sorry, I started it last Friday and it is now Wednesday.

I have considered phoning you but three thousand miles of telephone line costs a lot more than the usual 15 cents so I'm afraid it is out of the question. Possibly one day I'll find my way back to Phoenix again, but however much I'd like to, I know darn well that it's very unlikely that I'll ever see it again. All the same, I still can't quite realize that I'm never going to see you again, or dance with you again, or even speak to you over the telephone.

Tuesday 19th Y'know, for the first time in my life I'm stuck for something to say in a letter. It's well over a week now since I started it — I've mentally written six and just as mentally tore them up. The commissions have come through and we do nothing all day but eat and sleep, but it's still not finished. My trouble, child, as you probably guessed, is that I'm completely crazy about you — and have been for many moons. Oh I know, these things should be said in a suitably romantic atmosphere, and certainly not on paper, but — well, it's better this way. After all, even in the remote possibility of your feeling the same way I would still have had to leave with, as I said before, a very slim chance of ever coming back — and anyway, darling we did have fun, didn't we? I think if you recall various conversations you'll find I've explained my point of view before, and I'm sure you'll agree it made things easier, if not for both of us, at least for me. Anyway, I'd like to hear your views on the subject, though something tells me I've already heard them in these same conversations which, if my hunch is correct, were marvels of subtle tact and diplomacy! I'm sorry I've been so coldly analytical about a subject like this, but I'm afraid if I'm not I'll say an awful lot which would wreck everything. Anyway, let's forget it in future and make things horribly platonic. It shouldn't be hard in your case! Here we pause for a badly needed cigarette! Ten minutes later. Ah, that's much better! I think I'd had better close now, before I say anymore — I've said far too much already!

> So - G'night, baby,
> Sweet dreams, Eric

P.S. Don't write to me here, I may not get it in time. I think I gave you my home address, but if not, here it is: 154, London Road, Morden, Surrey, England

Ah, that's much better! I think I'd better close now, before I say anymore — I've said far too much already!

So - g'night, baby,
Sweet dreams,

Eric

CHAPTER SIX

Training Continues in England

Eric was first stationed at Harrogate, Yorkshire, for yet more training after which there was a series of training moves. During this time he wrote to Frances again but due to security he was not really able to tell her what he was doing. All letters were read by censors, so he had to be very discreet about what he wrote. No matter where Eric was he used his home address of 154 London Road, Morden, Surrey.

Tuesday March 22nd 1943

My Dearest Frances,

I imagine you'd given up hope of ever hearing from me again! Well there you have your first, and I hope, your last example of how bad the transatlantic mail service can be. It was I who gave up hope of hearing from you! In fact I had begun to wonder if my last letter had shocked you! However, your letter finally arrived, having been held up approximately eight weeks. Since then I have had no time at all to write. I'm working hard for a change. However, today your second letter arrived, and I decided I really must reply as soon as possible. I only have an hour before night ops — not the kind you're thinking of — so I'll probably have to finish this tomorrow. The trouble is I have no air mail stationery, and since I can only get into town at week-

ends, and this will be a very long letter, it will probably cost a small fortune in stamps. I've got so much gen for you that I don't know where to begin. First I think I'll go through both your letters — commenting suitably. So you've had your hair cut! To say the least I take a pretty dim view — it's almost sacrilege! However, it has one good point — if you have any left after all your admirers (who no doubt, are very numerous) have received a share, could you send me a lock of "Arizona sunshine." Ridiculously sentimental, I know, but I always was that way.

I am beginning to wonder if Adolf has sent another valuable cargo to the bottom of the Atlantic, in other words, your photograph hasn't yet arrived. Probably detailed a special U-boat to derail the morale of the R.A.F! I'm afraid there are no photographs of me to send at the moment. I hate having them taken, and always put it off as long as possible. However if you still want one I'll see what I can do about it. Next we come to a paragraph I will not remark on since we both seem to have agreed that the subject is taboo. Nevertheless, when I said "horribly platonic" I didn't expect you to take me quite so seriously — in fact I hoped you wouldn't. Contradictory sort of bloke aren't I?! (translating: bloke, chap, fellow) in case you still don't know the English. I'm afraid McKenna has sadly misled you. I've never even heard of the book you spoke about, and I certainly never saw the paper he said was tacked up in the lounge. I suggest you give him a good talking to and tell him Pilot Officer Hutchin takes a dim view of him teasing a poor innocent little girl, no doubt he'll be suitably impressed! So we come to the end of your first letter and I'm afraid I'll have to leave this till tomorrow. It's about time to go.

Till tomorrow then,
sweet dreams, darling,
Eric

Thursday

A short passage from your letter caused quite a stir in the mess. The bit about having to go indoors because it was too warm outside in the sun. Sorry, Mr. Censor, I forgot, no reference to the weather was allowed. Anyway Frances, there's no harm in saying that the weather here is all that you've been told it is — and then some. Boy! Give me Arizona! Glad to hear you've been studying Shakespeare. It'll improve your mind! However, I could suggest a more suitable play than "Hamlet" and if you don't get it ask Genevieve. (Incidentally "i" before or after "e"?) Why are you so modest about your singing? I seem to remember lying in bed for an hour on er — Christmas morning I believe, and listening to a very beautiful little private operatic performance, and there was certainly nothing wrong with it then. I was half asleep at the time, and until you told me you had been practicing I thought I had a wizard dream! Darned hard luck not getting the scholarship. Will you get another shot at it? 'Scuse me. I must refuel (though from the mistakes I've been making I've had enough already!) Beer, beer, glorious beer! (No I'm not tight!?

My dear girl, do you credit me with no intelligence at all!) You suggest that I might possibly have not heard of Paul Robeson and you dare to say that he is one of the greatest baritones of today. The greatest, please. The end of your letter – the G in my name stands for Geoffrey, like it? Before I leave your letter. You said in the first one you say you are going to try to not let me forget you. What on earth gave you the idea I was going to? Shall I tell you my greatest ambition at the moment? It is to complete my ops on fighters (safely I hope) and then, when we've wiped Germany off the map, to be posted to the States as C.O. at Falcon. After that, well that would remain to be seen. Rather a far-fetched daydream I know, but anyway I've a feeling that one day I'll turn up in Phoenix again like the proverbial bad penny. Well dear, I'm afraid it's once more time to go to bed – I'm the last one in the mess as it is. Eight pages so far (well sides anyway) and all I've done is talk about your letters. We'll get onto some gen tomorrow.

Hasta la luego, caro mío, Eric

Remember the reference to night ops? Well – as I said – it wasn't the kind you were thinking – flying. No, I'm afraid I haven't flown at all in this country yet. We are on the course McKenna told us about. If you don't remember he'll probably tell you anyway. I'm certainly not enjoying it – we might as well be in the infantry. It's supposed to make one fit and tough – personally, if that's fitness, I'd rather stay soft. However, we have to do it, and there's only a week left before we go back to our normal life of ease. I'm afraid I'm allowed to say very little about what I'm doing — we are supposed to keep off service subjects altogether, and there's been little else we can talk about I'm afraid.

I'll have to close soon. I had two weeks disembarkation leave after I got back, which I'm afraid was rather spoilt by the family, who had it all planned out every day to take me around the place shooting a horrible line to various, uninteresting relatives. Making polite conversation was never my strong point, and I would have been much happier cruising around the night clubs. Sorry, I forgot you disapproved of them! The family is still kicking hard as ever — one brother was married while I was in the States and when I saw him he was still in the throes of married bliss. The other brother is about to present me with my third niece, at least his wife is. My parents were very pleased to see me and boy! Was I spoiled? I hope I can say without getting censored that I've practically got the Spitfire. Three recommendations and three definite requests for fighters should do the trick! However I don't get on ops for some time yet, so I'm safe for a while!

Ian says you are to give up smoking or stay off the beer otherwise you will lose your voice entirely! Seems to have some queer ideas! Remember me to your family and wish Claude luck for me. Oh yes! Give my love to Jenny and tell her Ian will drop her a line sometime. Ian has just received a terrific epistle from Martha — a *collaborative effort written by her and five other girls at her college — it actually fills a book! Completely crazy of course, but what would you expect from Martha! Personally I am convinced the girl is quite mad! But I must go, write soon darling. But please not quite so platonic this time!*

> *Thine ever,*
> *fair lady,*
> *Eric*

After his disembarkation leave Eric was stationed "somewhere in the English countryside." It was evident that the beauty of the English spring had quite an impact after he had spent so many months in the arid Arizona desert. The following letter, written April 7th, 1943, describes that spring of 1943.

Friday, April 7th, 1943

Small note in corner:
PS: Bennett is still with us and wished to be remembered to you.

Frances darling, I have good news — the photograph arrived at last — undamaged after wandering around many R.A.F. stations before finally catching me up, but boy, it was sure worth waiting for! Frances dear, it's really marvelous — I can't describe my feelings when I first opened it up — quite honestly I had to look away and prepare for the next time. It seemed to give me a sort of hollow feeling in the region of my fourth rib, maybe I've lost something that should be there. Was it around? I believe I left it somewhere in

Phoenix! The photograph now reposes where I see it immediately I open the door of my room — I get the same sort of shock every time I get back to my room — even makes climbing stairs something to look forward to! The news of the entering of Bizerte by US troops and of Tunis by British troops has just come through on the radio — darn good show, what! I'm afraid I started this letter rather late tonight and I must away to bed. Like you, instead of writing I usually find my time day dreaming which doesn't get me anywhere but wastes a lot of time.

Buenos nochas, Eric

Here Eric has a small pencil drawing of a Spitfire obviously over Phoenix
(judging by the sun and Superstition Mountain)

Saturday 8th

Your letter arrived yesterday afternoon but also travelled fairly far — it took eighteen days to get here. They must have started the air mail service all the way again —how do you manage to fill so much space? Eight large closely written, very interesting pages — don't know how you do it. Presumably you'll get this a few days before you graduate — wish I could be there to see the fun. Anyway give me a special thought just before the ceremony — if only as the chap who nearly made you flunk an English test! If you see Mrs. McDowell again, say hello for both Ian and I and tell her we will write soon. How is Genevieve getting on — still spouting Shakespeare?! Are you still teaching her all you know about men or is the position reversed?

You asked if Ten Course was split up very much. Well, naturally I can't say much, but the sergeants (never could spell that) have all left us while the commissioned fellows are in two groups. There are three others with me (including Ian) and we seem to be staying together. With luck Ian and I should stay together — I hope so — we should make a good team since we know each other so well. It's almost got to the stage where we read each other's letters (don't worry I said almost!) By the way I now smoke a pipe! This is all that can be seen of me.

The fellow who said he saw Ian in Manchester caused quite a bit of trouble. Apparently Mrs. Day told Ian's beloved Marilynn, who immediately wrote a very nasty letter to the little lad complaining that he didn't write until long after he arrived in England. Anyway Ian immediately wrote back — it's just as nasty — and now we're waiting for the reply. I don't think his heart would be completely broken — he's pretty far gone on Martha now — in a crazy sort of way — it's just as well he didn't get that way before, our country couldn't hold those two! The part of England I am in at the moment (not far away — I'm moving again very soon) is entirely different to my home, as you know I live on the outskirts of London, a city man, and now I'm in quite a small town in the country. The surrounding country is very nice — it's a well known beauty spot — but I can't hope to describe it to you. Better seen there — I have tried — and failed — to write about England in the springtime, and it has to be seen to be appreciated. The most striking thing about England, especially after having lived in Arizona, a land of browns and yellows — is the brilliant green of the countryside. When we left the boat and travelled by train to the country, even we were amazed at the bright emerald green of the grass, and the thousands of other shades in the trees and the hedges — all fresh and sort of dewy. Where the land is plowed, the soil is of such a rich brown that it appears almost red. The fields, by American standards, are so small as to appear rather ridiculous, so that from the air it looks like an immense patchwork quilt. Another thing you would notice — birds, thousands of them — and all singing — entirely unlike anything in Arizona. This part of the country is made up of rolling wooded hills covered with small farms and little old towns, most of which have histories dating back to the days of the border wars of the English and Scots, and all the centuries old churches and castles — it's more or less the "castled" part of England. You'd like it — if you could stand the climate! Sorry about the mistakes in the last few pages — I'm definitely not good at this sort of thing but you asked me to tell you what it was like, however I didn't intend to get quite so poetic. You asked another question — about rather a ticklish subject — at least it is to you; to us it's as normal as it gets — almost callous — as you may remember. Anyway if anything does happen you will hear about it from three sources in the Air Ministry who send a telegram to anyone we name; for myself when we get on ops, we write letters to be sent if we "don't come back" and from my people or possibly a friend on the same squadron who has the lousy job of explaining what happened to relatives or friends — it's usually the C.O. However the question won't come up until I'm on ops — not for some time. Well darling, I'm afraid I must get some sleeping hours in and anyway I finished up my supply of stationery. Please write again soon,

all my love
Eric

P.S. The radio is playing "When the Lights Go on Again," remember? It always makes me think of you.

P.P.S. I do anyway.

A photograph Frances
sent to Eric

Eric in flying gear

By now Eric was a Flying Officer, deep in training in the English countryside gaining his first experience learning to fly the legendary Hurricane aircraft. He was pretty much confined to the aerodrome, as is evident in a letter to Frances written on June 15th, 1943.

Wednesday June 15, 1943   (Hmm, I find it should be Tuesday)

Dearest,

You seem to have a flair for finding wizard cards — first the one sent with the photographs, and now this effort. I must agree. It's a very good likeness — at least you also have freckles, and big, round innocent eyes, but surely your hair is not so long you have to wear it in plaits! And if you dyed it black I'll never speak to you again! Incidentally, I believe your last letter caused some neglect of English — it seems to have had a bad effect! To quote — "I haven't hardly seen him since" — but don't worry, I've corrected it for you! However there is a more serious side to this. It seems I have unwittingly ruined your social life in Phoenix — you remember how surprised I was when you told me no fellow in Phoenix would date you in case they should step on "his" toes (I've forgotten his name — believe it's Ralph). However, I've told you how things are in England, so you'll understand why I don't quite get it — by our standards the "other guests" who would have watched you and your partner very carefully, would be, to say the least, rather narrow minded! However, having lived in Phoenix for a year, I think I understand.

You seemed to be in doubt as to whether you were a "good child" or not — my dear, you are neither — you're not a child at all anymore. Possibly you are lacking in years and experience, but your letters show that you make up for them in what I believe is known as "woman's wisdom of the years." Anyway, you're eighteen now and getting quite a big girl! Yes, I did remember your birthday — it's next Tuesday, June 21st, (sorry next Monday.) I remembered it a month ago, but I've been unable to get into any big town for well over a month— transport is practically non-existent over here now, and I'm stationed miles from anywhere in the heart of the country. I haven't even been able to get to a post office to send a cable, so even that will probably be late. (Very appropriately the radio is playing "Don't Get Around Much Anymore.") However, I've had lots of time for thought. And I've had what I consider to be a stroke of genius. You see, it's practically impossible to obtain anything interesting in the way of birthday presents, but after racking my brains for several days I hit on a wizard scheme — I assure you it will be absolutely unique — especially in Phoenix, and I think you'll like it. I won't be able to get it till I go to London again, but I'll send it as soon as possible, so you must be able to contain your curiosity for a while.

As you will realize, since I never leave the aerodrome and I can't tell you anything I do here, there's very little I can tell you, anyway, it's long past my bedtime and I must leave this until tomorrow night. While I remember it however, I'd like you to give the boys at

Falcon a little advice — learnt from bitter experience. The first is on cross country's — tell 'em to pinpoint every inch of the way, and steer accurate courses — also to practice estimating courses if they are going on fighters. The next thing is to learn to use their mixture control to the best advantage otherwise they'll be "one of our aircraft failed to return!!" You, of course can't make head or tail of all that, but I suggest you tell Wing Commander McKenna to repeat it to them — those are the two things flying in Arizona tends to make one forget. Suggest that the rhyme — to maintain required airspeed: " Low revs and high boost, will bring you safely home to roost" — should be posted in the flight office.

I don't think I've given anything away there, Mr. Censor.
Buenos noches muchacha.   Eric

Tuesday night
I'm starting on this again, but I haven't the least idea of what I'm going to write about. The only thing I do is fly, and that, as I've said, is a forbidden subject. Let's reminisce (correct spelling?). Remember the hayride? Remember the rose you wore in your hair? (Sounds like a song title!) You thought you'd lost it, but you hadn't. I didn't dare tell you then, but it was in my pocket when we were looking for it — I've still got it — a few dry, crumpled petals. Well I warned you I was too darned sentimental! You didn't tell me how the graduation went. Wish I'd been there. What do you intend to do now? College? If so, I can recommend the Eng-

lish Universities — their courses usually last five years! However, if you ever did come over here, I assure you, you wouldn't spend five years at college! It's no good, inspiration has deserted me. I'll have to try making notes of everything I do that might interest you and crowd that into a letter. May be something in this diary business after all! Talking of diaries, I wonder if you'd tell me what's in your diary for 1-1-43? Bet you won't! I'm afraid I've completely run out of ideas — but I'll write again next week. Y'know, it's no good waiting for each other's letters before we reply — they don't arrive often enough. Let's write every week or so— your letters are worth their weight in gold to me you know.

Excuse the half sheet — there's a paper shortage over here. 'Scuse also the writing — that's incurable — and the change of ink — my pen just ran out. Anyway I've only got to finish off. Give my love to your family and anyone else you can think of who is worthy (!) of it. Goodnight darling,

Hasta la vista,
all my love,
Eric

CHAPTER SEVEN

Reminiscing and "Hopelessly in Love"

Following yet another promotion on July 1, 1943, Eric was still gaining experience flying the Hurricane aircraft before being assigned to the Operational No. 1 Squadron based at Lympne, Kent. By this time Eric makes it obvious as to how much in love with Frances he is.

Flying Officer E.G. Hutchin,

Thursday 9th September 1943

My Dearest Frances,
No doubt you are wondering — I'm sorry darling, but this time the blame must be carried on the broad shoulders of the jolly old British Post Office. It's the first time I've known them to slip up, and they had to choose your letters. But let me begin at the end. Today I received a very important official looking envelope addressed c/o The Air Ministry with "On His Majesty's Service" in large letters across the top. At first I thought they had caught up with me at last! Inside was the card and letter that you posted on July 2nd and 3rd...it seems that the dimwits at our local Post Office at home had read the "4" in "154" as "7" and returned them with

"No such number" and "Unknown return to sender" written on the envelope. However, someone had the sense to send them to the Air Ministry and they, kind souls, got them through to me inside a week. Not bad considering the number of chaps there are in the R.A.F. Anyway I intended to send a snooty letter to the Post Office about it — admittedly it could be taken for a "7" but, oh well, it's beyond me.

I trust you have already noted my change in rank — it's equivalent to getting the silver bar in the U.S. Army — in other words I am a "full" lieutenant. I can't pretend it's because of any great ability on my part, it's automatic after we've been commissioned six months. All the same it's rather nice — it carries more pay, so I'm not complaining. The only difference in my uniform is that the thin blue line around my sleeve gets a trifle thicker — it wouldn't be noticeable in the photograph. Oh yes, the photographs. Personally (and Ian agrees with me) I think it's lousy. There is a coloured version which was intended for you, but they gave it such a horribly yellowed complexion that it looks more like something the canary frightened than me — at least, I hope it does. Actually the photographer did a pretty good job considering the poor material he had to work on. Anyway I hope you like it.

Excuse me, I must take time out for food. I saw a wizard movie yesterday. It was called "Tomorrow We Live" and was all about the French underground movement — anyway — in the middle of the program they flashed a notice on the screen — "Italy has capitulated" — there was sort of stunned silence at first — then there came the most terrific yell of delight I've ever heard — the audience went crazy including me of course. Later the fellow I was with and I went over to the pub across the road to join a party of other persons who were celebrating the news. Maybe that doesn't mean much to you, but then you've never seen a crowd of R.A.F pilots with a really good cause for celebrating! Until you have your education is definitely incomplete! The result of all this was that we missed the last bus back to camp. Since all the hotels were full we were in rather a spot, but after wandering around town for a while we happened on the Police Station...! The boys at the station were most friendly, but that didn't make the cell bed any more comfortable! Believe me I know crime does not pay. I'm afraid this letter has been neglected for some time — in the middle of it I was told I was leaving my last station and going on leave. That meant two or three days of packing and doing all the things one had to do when one leaves a unit. Unluckily I packed all my writing materials and sent all my luggage by rail — they didn't arrive until this afternoon. Today, by the way is September 16th and I'm writing this at home, gloriously at ease in civvies with an extremely loud tie acquired in Phoenix.

I've just found that the letter you were referring to — you called it "disconnected", was the one which "brought the sunshine back into my life" — darling, I found nothing wrong with it. But then even if your letters consisted of just one line I still wouldn't complain. I shall never cease to wonder why you write at all — you know I shall never be worthy of you. Ian put it very well when he said "why a marvelous girl like that should fall for a dim clod like you is beyond me!" It's beyond me too but I'm not complaining — I hope you don't think because I don't seem to write very often that I'm forgetting you — on the contrary I fall more and more hopelessly in love with you every day, and I mean hopelessly. We have been rather busy lately and anyway I always was a lazy correspondent but I pay for it by feeling permanently guilty! Occasionally I think there's no future in it all, and feel horribly miserable for days — but I suppose it's best to keep ones thoughts in the past and present and leave the future to look after itself. I'm afraid I must leave this again darling. It's half past one in the morning and I'm so tired, I'm beginning to say things I shouldn't say. I have both our photographs on the table before me, mine is folded round the back side of yours so that it looks like a double mounting — and it's putting all sorts of strange ideas into my head — ideas which I dare not even consider, but which are rather wonderful all the same. I really must go now — I hope I dream of you! Goodnight Frances darling, and remember I do still love you even if I can't find the right words,

Adios, Eric

Sunday

My brother is home on leave — first time I've seen him for two years — since then he — or rather his wife has presented me with yet another niece, that makes me three times an uncle. Makes me feel quite old! You know I wish I could return cards like the ones you send, unluckily though, those things are practically unobtainable in England, I'm afraid this year's Christmas cards will be rather poor compared with last years' — remember the one I sent you? Hmm, talking about Christmas already — I wonder what it will be like this year. Somehow I think I shall spend it sitting in a corner dreaming about Christmas 1942. I wonder if we will ever spend another Christmas like that. Possibly the colour didn't quite match "our song" but all the same it was the happiest few days I ever spent. By the way you seem to be rather indignant because I thought you wouldn't know what that advice to cadets was all about — well dare I quote your own card back to you — "Don't know much about propellers, Or landing gear and such."

Now I must close. This letter may appear a little disjointed — it's been written in a series of short bits and pieces spread over a week. However for me it's a really marvellous effort — six pages. Nothing to you of course but to me it's quite a feat. I'll try to write again soon, though there is seldom very much to report when I'm on leave — I stay in bed most of the time.

Goodnight my darling, all my love, Eric

P.S. We both seem to have forgotten that we agreed to write platonic letters— well let's carry on forgetting — I *don't think I'd like it now!*

P.P.S. I trust the — er — birthday present has arrived by now — tell me if it hasn't.

Goodnight, my darling,
All my love,
Eric.
P.S. We both seem to have forgotten that we agreed to write platonic letters — well, let's carry on forgetting — I don't think I'd like it now!
P.P.S. I trust the — er — birthday present has arrived by now — tell me if it hasn't.

The following letter was undated but seems to have been written around the time that Frances graduated from high school. There was no envelope so it appears to have been included with a graduation gift.

Pilot Officer Hutchin

My Dearest Frances,
I'm afraid it's a little late, but I think I can be forgiven for that. You see, I had to go to London to get it, and leave has been very scarce since we got back to England. I hope you'll like it — at least there won't be another like it in Phoenix, and I don't think there's one in England. Old Mac (Wing Commander McKenna to you!) will probably recognize the wings — I be-

lieve they used to go on the R.A.F. evening dress before the war.

Thanks for the curly lock — when I opened your letter Ian was around and it fell out on the table before I realized it was there. I blushed a fiery red (much to his delight — the worm!) and tried to explain it. You can imagine how I felt! By the way, why, on the graduation invitation (for which, also, gracias), do "they" call it graduation "commencement exercises"? Surely it should be something like "finishing exercises." Apparently I still don't know the American language! Incidentally I'm awfully sorry I couldn't accept the invitation — wartime restrictions you know, and somehow the C.O. couldn't see my point when I explained why I wanted eight weeks leave! (Or should that be furlough?) I'm afraid I must go to bed now dear, this letter won't be very long as I shall post it with the parcel. I'll write a longer one afterwards — possibly I'll wait for your next letter, it should be here very shortly. However, I'll try to add a little to this tomorrow before I post it.

Goodnight darling, Eric

P.S. Sorry I can't write any more — and apologies for the packing — even that is hard to get in England! Eric XX

Eric was still moving around to various training postings and was gaining experience flying the legendary Hurricane. In November 1943 he sent a Royal Air Force Christmas card to Frances followed by a letter from "somewhere in Scotland."

On the card he wrote:

In memory of last Christmas — and in hope that there may be many more like it — I send you all my love, my darling — Eric

On the back:
Not, I'm afraid, quite like the last one I sent you — but the idea's there — Eric

GREETINGS AND ALL GOOD WISHES
FOR CHRISTMAS
AND THE NEW YEAR.

Tuesday, 23rd November 1943

Actually I'm in my room at a R.A.F camp "somewhere in Scotland" — and Scotland in winter is a very differ-ent place from Arizona, however a roaring fire beside me helps matters somewhat.

My dearest Frances,

I'm afraid I have been an awfully long time decid-ing to write again. I've no excuse either except that I'm like that. I occasionally have a burst of efficiency and clear up all my mail then I let it slide for weeks until there is an absolutely horrifying stack of letters waiting to be answered, however you remember what I said in my last letter? I hope your father enjoyed being mothered by you, some people seem to get all the luck. I shall have to get his views on your cooking, especially apple cobbler (whatever is apple cobbler anyway)? You certainly have all my sympathy, getting up at 5:45 am isn't exactly my idea of a holiday though you seem to enjoy it. Ever since I received your letter I have been in a state of perpetual impatience, hanging around the mailbox every day looking for the Falcon magazine. It hasn't arrived yet but it can't be long now.

Tell me, did you ever hear anything more about the book McKenna was teasing you about just after I left? The one with the name of cadets and their girlfriends and suitable comments in it? If you can get a look at it I'd love to hear anything about me, or rather us. I was rather glad I wasn't there when AVM Medhearst came down — anything higher than a wing commander usually fills me with such awe that I beat a hasty retreat — and if they catch me in a corner and speak to me — well things like floors opening up are definitely in order, you, however were merely "quite thrilled" the nerve of the girl. You know when the American soldiers come back they are going to find it quite hard to find a girl who isn't married to an R.A.F. fellow. It rather amused me the other day to see in the paper that several of a new contingent of W.A.A.C's who had arrived in the country were to be married to a R.A.F. boyfriend who had met them while training in the States. What is it that is so irresistible about American girls? One of our boys who trained at Lancaster Field has just met his girlfriend over here. When he left she joined the W.A.A.F's (American Women's Auxiliary Air Force) at the British Consulate in L.A. and arrived in England about six months after he did so presumably another wedding is on the way.

I can assure you Frances that the cell door was not locked, but it might well have been for all the sleep I got that night. I'm afraid I can't send a snap of myself in civvies darling, it's three years since I wore them for anything other than a few days at a time and I was rather young then, however I'll see what I can do for you on my next leave. There is however another photograph taken in uniform which I'll send as soon as I can "acquire" an envelope large enough. After all if you like the last one you'll like almost anything. At present it carries a moustache. I pencilled it in just to see what it would look like and decided not to grow one. It reminded me of one of the granddaddies of all wolves, but maybe you think I look like that anyway. I'm sure Jenny does. I imagine she takes a rather dim view of me these days doesn't she?

I'm sorry to say Ian and I have now parted. He was posted to another station a short while ago so I'm afraid I've lost my artist. We may get together again of course but I imagine it is highly unlikely. Now I'm afraid whenever I want to illustrate my letters I'll have to do it myself. I've just discovered the secret of your long letters. You get exactly half as many words on one page as I do. So if you were writing this you would just be completing the seventh side, ah, that's eased my conscience considerably. A pal of mine, who is unluckily dead, once described my writing as "microscopically-Eric-like." Now I know what he meant. Sorry about the blot. I'm afraid I must close for tonight. It's very late and I have to be up early too! Goodnight my darling — see you tomorrow. Eric

It's rather late already 11:45 pm but I'm determined to finish this off tonight. Unluckily I was orderly officer today — nothing to it but saying "Carry on sergeant" and signing one's name on dozens of different forms which people keep pushing under one's nose. "Would you mind signing this sir," "Hmm? Oh certainly, everything under control corporal?" Yes sir, right carry on," and so it goes on. Nothing to do but it keeps me up late. N.C.O's are the backbone of this Air Force. All an officer needs to know is how to sign his name.

Have you ever heard of "Screwball Beurling"? He's a Canadian fighter pilot who is one of the war's most amazing aces, his skill as a pilot, his amazing eyesight and his deadly accurate shooting have become legendary in the last two years, especially when he was in Malta. Well, anyway I was reading his life story the other day and I came across McKenna's name. Apparently he (Mac) was C.O. at Beurling's flying school in Canada and one day he caught Beurling low flying. He chased him for some time but Screwball managed to keep his tail towards Mac and lost him. Had he managed to get his number of course, McKenna would have washed him out and we would have lost one of our best fighter pilots. Now you have something to tease Mac about.

My elder brother has just been posted to Canada. He's on ground staff at a station in Alberta quite near the border. I felt quite a veteran when I read his first letters. They were mainly about food, lack of blackouts, your fiendish train whistles etc. although he's ten years older than me I felt as if I was watching a small brother growing up. Most amusing. I can assure you of course my next letter will be on a rather superior note giving him a few tips from an old hand and telling him what to do and what not to do. In fact I shall enjoy it as much as he will. I must say I rather envy him. If I ever get posted there on instructing or something I'll get lost on my first flight and somehow find myself running short of gas over Sky Harbor. (Incidentally that should be "Harbour.") Then of course a fast street and well...I'm sure the other pupils at Junior College would find it most entertaining. My imagination is conjuring up all sorts of delightful life dreams but they must remain dreams for the moment I'm afraid. One day however... but this is not good enough.

Let's change the subject. Hmm, there doesn't seem to be any more subjects to change to except that now it's 12:45 am and my pen won't seem to do what I want it to. By the way the guardian angel you sent me has turned my little single seater into a two seater job. I would as soon think about flying without him as without my aeroplane. Anyway he's bound to bring me luck. Remember what the gypsy said? A blue eyed blonde I believe, as well as all sorts of gongs, long life and bags of shekels. Hope she was right. Darling, I really must close now, or all the guardian angels in the world aren't going to keep my awake when I'm flying tomorrow, and it doesn't do to go to sleep!

Goodnight sweetheart,
   I love you — always, Eric

CHAPTER EIGHT

Will You Marry Me?

The war was still having a profound effect on life in England and everything was in short supply, even writing paper was becoming difficult to find. However, Eric always managed to find enough paper (even stationery brought home from Falcon Field) so that he could pour his heart out to Frances. Frances had sent him some "wizard" stationary he really liked!

Friday, 31st, December 1943

My Dearest Frances,
Like the first letter I wrote to you I'm finding it rather difficult to know what to say — but I must first of all thank you for this wizard stationery — I'm quite sure nothing else like it has been seen in England for many years. The stuff we get over here nowadays is really awful — it's either like sandpaper or blotting paper — and airmail stationery is so thin that practically all that goes in the envelope is the ink —! As you've probably noticed, I've been using one of the Falcon writing packs since I got home — with the crest cut off, of course.

And then, of course, there was the "Falcon." To quote your last letter — "I thought you might like a copy."

You know darling, with your flair for understatement you could almost pass for English. Might like it! Quite frankly, I almost wept (!) when I read it — it made me feel more homesick than I've ever been before — I read it at home (I'm on leave at the moment) and luckily no-one else was in, so I could make all sorts of noises to myself, eventually I spent about half an hour talking to your photograph. I've caught myself doing that quite a lot lately — you must be driving me crazy — there's a most mischievous look in your eyes just now — stop looking at me like that! You see how you've got me! The wolf at bay! Woof! Woof! But this is getting me nowhere — I'm just playing for time. You're scared Eric old boy. Well and who wouldn't be?

Let's be serious. To be blunt darling, I — er —I'm going to — er — propose! Oh I know. You've always dreamed of a romantic proposal in the moonlight with soft lights and sweet music as a background — shall we say in a canoe on Encanto Park Lake — my idea of the perfect setting — but I'm afraid that just at the moment that would be rather hard to arrange. Probably you disapprove of a proposal by air mail — well believe me, so do I, and I'd give my right arm to be able to do the job properly, but — well, there's a war on, and I guess this is just one more thing we can blame Adolf for. Of course there are several "ifs". (Unconditional surrender? Never, sir, by gad!)

There is, of course, the possibility — but let's not think of that. Shall we say that if I can possibly get back to

Phoenix (or if you can come over here) then, darling, will you marry me?

There is, of course, the possibility — but let's not think of that. Shall we say that if I can possibly get back to Phoenix (or if you can come over here) then, darling, will you marry me?

I need hardly say that I have no prospects whatsoever — my education was interrupted by this darn war and by the time I get out of the R.A.F. I'll be too old to try starting again where I left off. All I can do is fly — I can't do that very well either — you ask Mac — in fact all I can offer you is me — not much is it? I can't give you anything but love, baby, that's the only thing I've plenty of — very true! I won't try the old line about "living on love" or "two can live as cheaply as one" — I'll give you credit for having heard that before! I'm sorry, darling, I realize I should treat this more seriously but I've got to cover up my nervousness and embarrassment somehow. After all, some unlucky censor is going to read this! Hard luck, old man! To come back to earth — I've been daydreaming as usual — the time is 2:40 am — on January 1st 1944. Our first anniversary — mind if I call it that? But nevertheless, time I went to bed. Goodnight Frances. Darling — I suggest you put this down for a while to recover — it shakes me!

8:20 am — still 1st January. Let's see — it should be 2:20 pm in Phoenix — just a year since I got my wings.

And in two hours time — forgive me if I have the times wrong, but I don't keep a diary, and I lost all count of time on that day. I had planned a little surprise for you today — I was going to cable some flowers (roses, red roses), but a sympathetic government cancelled the service the day before I got there — nice of 'em wasn't it? Tell me darling, why did we have to wait until my last day — it didn't give us much time did it? We should have met long before, you know — just think of the fun we could have had together with an extra three months.

Have I ever told you of the first time I saw you? It was the first weekend we spent in Phoenix — there had been a water polo match between Falcon and Williams (we beat 'em up too). Afterwards there was dancing on the tennis courts at the same place — I think it was the university swimming pool and sports field. Anyway, I was dancing with Martha and wondering if all American girls were as crazy, when we passed two girls watching the dancing. One was a beautiful blonde, blue eyed vision in white, the other, who I'm afraid I didn't notice — was Jenny. Martha of course said "hello Sissy" and I of course thought she meant you. Afterwards, when I pushed off to look for you, you'd both disappeared. Now, if only you'd stayed there five minutes longer —! For weeks after that I drove Martha almost crazy insisting she had another sister. Possibly my description was a little too colourful for her to recognize you, though personally I think it was rather conservative. After that it took me three months to find you again. A good show all around — but I found you eventually, and I suppose that's all that matters now.

By the way, if you look at the two photographs of the AT on the last but one page of the "Falcon" I think you'll find that the chap in BP213 is me, sorry, is I. The rest of the family seem to be quite sure, but just in case, could you check up and find out when the photographs were taken and by whom? If it is me the photographer will probably be Mr. Klatha — an instructor at Falcon at the time. Unluckily I haven't my log book with me at the moment, so I can't check on the nites I did my formation in the AT's.

Well, darling, there's just three minutes of January 1st left, and the year since I saw you is almost over, although, of course, it's only six o'clock in Phoenix. Somehow it seems impossible that twelve months have passed since the last time I hitched my way back to Mesa. Was it really a year ago that I kissed you good-bye and wended my blissfully unhappy way towards the "hub"? (That sounds rather ambiguous, I know, but I think you'll understand.)

Let's see, just now we would be having supper — you were facing me across the table — you were very silent, looking awfully shy and demure — and very sweet. I was trying to keep up a polite conversation with your mother and father — probably saying the most ridiculous things, but not caring anyway. You know — it must have looked rather obvious to them — I don't think we made a great success of concealing our feelings. That reminds me — does your mother approve of me now? I believe there was a time when I wasn't very popular with her, remember? I hope she doesn't think of me as a big bad wolf!

I never seem to tell you anything about what I'm doing — just as well I suppose, and anyway it would probably all be censored. However, I don't think there's any harm in telling you that I'm flying Typhoons at the moment — my beloved Spitfire didn't materialize, I'm afraid. However, I think the Tiffie is just as good, though she's an ugly brute compared with the beautiful Spit. Well, I guess that's all for now — this has been quite a letter hasn't it? I must admit I'm glad I've got it written — I felt so nervous when I started it as if I was going to propose properly — I'll do that too, I hope — sometime. Now I shall spend the next few weeks haunting the mail base and dogging the footsteps of every postman I see. Please don't keep me in suspense too long!

Goodnight Frances,
I love you my darling, always, Eric

Eric wrote to Frances in March 1944, while home on leave, still making reference to his marriage proposal and obviously trying to come to terms with the futility of daring to dream during times of war.

Wednesday, March 28th, '44

My Dearest Frances,
So you had difficulty in writing your letter! Darling, you don't know the half of it! So far I've made just six attempts — all of them just wandered off into nothing — leaving me with my brain reeling (sounds rather dramatic, but I still feel that way — and I still don't know what I'm going to say.) Now I intend to attempt to collect the scattered fragments of my reason and write an ordinary letter, skipping comments on the all important question while I — so to speak — am not looking.

I hope you will not be too shocked when I tell you that all I know about music could be written on a postage stamp and still leave room for its gum — in fact I know precisely nothing except that I often hear things I rather like but of which I can seldom remember the names. I believe I once thought Handel's "Water Music" was rather nice — and isn't there something called "The Dance of the Swans" from some ballet or other? Actually, my choice of records would consist of practically nothing but waltzes — "Tales from the Vienna Woods," "Invitation to the Waltz," "The Emperor Waltz," and so on. Stick to Johann and you can't go wrong!

It's 12:15 am and the air raid warning has just

sounded. The London blitz (1944 series) is quite exciting — definitely more so than the 1940 type — though why the Hun doesn't use his aircraft to better purpose is quite beyond me. Incidentally, don't believe what "they" tell you about the Luftwaffe being out of action — you'd know why if you were here just now. As you'll have gathered, I'm at home on leave at the moment — that's why I'm not using the stationery you sent me — I'm afraid I left it back at camp. This stuff is all that remains of the Falcon notepaper — with the letterhead cut off. (By the way, my writing is more than unusually foul tonight, don't you think?) "Now's the time, old boy." "Do you really think so?" "Sure. He's not looking this way." "O.K."

To quote from your letter — "American women have always been allowed so much more freedom than women in other countries —!!" Frances! Frankly, I could hardly believe my eyes when I read that. So you honestly think that English women enjoy a lesser degree of freedom than American women? Because if you do I can assure you that you are very, very wrong. Just now, possibly, the word doesn't mean an awful lot in England, but then, there's a war on! I can assure you that in peace-time there is very little to choose between the two countries. Presumably you are thinking of the conscription of women for the Services and for war work — if so, then I don't think you realize how desperate the situation in England was in 1940. Our population, you know, is less than one third of yours and only one half that of Germany — that meant we were outnumbered by two to one, without taking into consideration the lack of sufficient war materials and trained men. Something had to be done to release more men and to produce more munitions, so they conscripted women. Surely that doesn't mean English women are less free than Americans — but I suppose you must take my word for it until you can see for yourself. While we're on the subject — you mentioned that you felt I would not be willing to leave England. Frances, darling, I don't want to sound too sentimental, but wherever you are, that's home to me. You can go and live at the North Pole if you like — I'll follow and let a seal marry us — we'll live on polar bear and whale meat. We wouldn't need a fire, anyway. After all, I wouldn't exactly be creating a precedent for Englishmen in living outside England. Apart from those two points, you were, of course, right in everything you said. Don't think I condemn you for it — on the contrary, I should never have proposed to you in the first place — though I know I'd do it again, crazy or not. If it was possible — and of course, if you agreed, I'd marry you tomorrow without thinking twice about it, although I'm all against war marriages — when a man is as much in love as I am he doesn't do anything much in the sensible way. I understand how you feel, because when I stop to think I feel the same way myself, but one rather tends to get out of the habit of stopping to think in my job. If another fellow asked my advice on the same problem I would probably tell him just what you've told me — and argue for hours that I was right — but that, I'm afraid, doesn't make things any easier.

Now I must dash off to bed — it's 1:30 am and the effort of the last two pages has made me reach the same abysmal depths of misery as when I first read your letter. Maybe that's rather exaggerated, but sensible or not, I am very disappointed (now I've gone to the other extreme of understatement, but at least I'm tired.) Before I leave this for tonight — tell me: if all conditions had been perfect — would you have said "yes"?

On reading it over, that doesn't look so good either — this is one of the few occasions when I think I could explain myself better if I could talk to you. Somehow, however, I think if we were together again I'd see everything in an entirely different light — I'd be proposing every second sentence! I think we'll leave it at that.

Ian seems to be enjoying life fairly well — I haven't seen him since last November. When we do meet again I imagine there'll be quite a party.

I believe I promised you a photograph some time back — I couldn't send it because I'd been trying the effect of a moustache on it. Sorry, I didn't know you disliked them so much! Anyway, the shrubbery has now been removed so I'll send it as soon as I find an envelope to fit it.

I have recently received a very fat income tax refund, with the result that my bank balance is looking very healthy, so healthy that I intend to buy me a car. That's quite an event these days, you know — operational pilots are the only people (apart from doctors, etc) who can get any petrol — sorry, gasoline. Even so, we only get 550 miles a quarter — not much, but enough to pop into the next town without worrying how one is to get back. The only trouble seems to be getting insured — most companies seem to consider fighter pilot's cars too big a risk!

Yesterday I took my mother for a row on the Thames — most unusual for me to be taking voluntary exercise, I can assure you! It was quite good fun, but I'm afraid my mother has very few clues on how to row — or, for that matter, on how to steer when I'm rowing. She nearly turned us over once!

Since I wrote the first page, I've thought of two more suggestions — "Destiny Waltz" and "Rustle of Spring" — by a guy named Sinding. Hope they meet with your approval. There, I'm afraid I must leave you — it's midnight again, and I haven't been getting enough sleep.

Goodnight dearest,
All my love,
Eric

P.S. Can one still make records of one's voice in the States? I believe there were places where it could be done when I was there. If so — I hardly like to ask you — could you — or, rather, would you, please, sing some-

thing onto a disk and send it to me? I've only heard you sing once, you know, you and Barbara Creighton gave Ian and I your version of some Christmas Carols — it was at the end of a Christmas party. I leave the choice of song to you — I know it will be something very appropriate if you choose it. Consider it anyway.

Love, Eric

CHAPTER NINE

Spitfires, Typhoons and 182 Squadron

Eventually Eric was posted to 182 Squadron along with his best friend, Ian, with whom he had trained at Falcon Field. Towards the end of 1943 he was flying a Typhoon although he desperately wanted to fly a Spitfire, a plane he described as "the best little aeroplane in the world." In March 1944 he switched to a Spitfire and then alternated between the two aircraft. Pilots likened flying the Typhoon to flying a tank after the nimble "Spit."

The Spitfire is the most famous British fighter aircraft in history. It became a symbol of freedom during the summer months of 1940 by helping to defeat the German air attacks during the Battle of Britain. It was the highest performing Allied aircraft in 1940.

The crowds at the 1936 RAF Display at Hendon had a first glimpse of the prototype Spitfire in the New Types Park but it was not until August 1938 that production Spitfires began to enter service. By the outbreak of war, a year later, nine squadrons were equipped. In spite of vigorous demands from the French the Commander in Chief of Fighter Command refused to send any Spitfires to France during the German Blitzkrieg of 1940. The wisdom of that decision was clearly shown. By July 1940 RAF Fighter Command had nineteen Spitfire MkI squadrons available.

The other love of Eric's life.
Courtesy Wikipedia

Once the RAF modified their tactics to properly counter the Luftwaffe, the Spitfire Mk I proved to be the only British fighter capable of meeting the Messerschmitt Bf109E on equal terms. Often the outcome of a combat depended more on the quality of the pilot than his aircraft.

Information courtesy Andrew Simpson, Curator of the Department of Aircraft and Exhibitors, Royal Air Force Museum, Hendon, England • www.rafmuseum.org

The following extracts, used by permission of the authors, provide pilots' appreciations of the two aircraft, Spitfires and Typhoons, and also give us a good idea of what Eric's life was like in the air — information censors would have redacted from his letters to Frances.

182 SQUADRON
From www.historyofwar.org, courtesy of Dr. John Rickard

No.182 Squadron was formed on 25 August 1942 at Martlesham Heath. In September 1942 Nos. 181 and 182 Squadrons received bomb armed Typhoons, and went onto the offensive. The Typhoon began to come into its own as a ground attack aircraft during 1943. Day and night the increasing number of Typhoon squadrons launched attacks on the German transport system in occupied France, becoming adept at destroying railway trains. This was a dangerous duty, operating at low level against defended targets, and 380 Typhoons were lost during 1943 (many to flak). During the same period the Typhoon shot down 103 German aircraft, including 52 of the formidable FW 190s.This was an impressive record for an aircraft that was considered to have failed as an interceptor.

Research during 1943 would prepare the Typhoon for its moment of glory in 1944. Tests confirmed that the bomb load could be increased to 1000lb under each wing, making it the first fighter to carry such a high bomb load. Perhaps more importantly, the Typhoon was cleared to carry rocket projectiles. The normal payload consisted of eight rockets, although that could be doubled by the use of a specially designed two level rocket rack. The first rocket attack was made by Typhoons of No. 181 Squadron, against Caen power station on 25th October, 1943.

The Typhoon's moment of glory came during and after D-Day [6th June] in 1944 . The introduction of the Hawker Tempest allowed the Typhoon squadrons to concentrate entirely on their ground attack role. Eighteen of the RAF's twenty Typhoon squadrons were allocated to the 2nd Tactical Air Force. Their first task was to destroy the German radar net in Normandy. On the days before D-Day Typhoon squadrons destroyed several crucial radar stations, including the station at Jobourg that covered the Normandy beaches. Once the landings had begun, the Typhoons turned to tactical support.The Normandy countryside was perfect for defensive tank warfare. A single German tank dug in behind the high hedges of the bocage country could seriously delay the Allied advance. The standard response was to call in air support, and let a rocket armed Typhoon take out the stubborn Panzer.

By the end of June the Typhoon squadrons had relocated to France, allowing them to increase the speed with which they could respond to calls for assistance. A crucial development was the use of the "Cab Rank" or "Taxi Rank" system. This involved maintaining a standing patrol of Typhoons over the battlefield. Below them would be a Forward Air Controller, whose job it was to direct the Typhoons onto the most important target at any moment. Once a target was identified, a stream of Typhoons would descend on it. This system came into its own during the battle of the Falaise pocket (14-25 August). This saw the German 7th Army almost encircled around Falaise. Only one narrow escape route remained. The Typhoon played a crucial role in blocking the route, destroying bridges, blocking roads and devastating German armoured formations. The dominating image of the final German collapse in France is of rockets streaking from a Typhoon towards German armour.

The Typhoon squadrons were heavily involved as the fighting moved towards Germany. During the Battle of the Bulge, they played an important part in the Allied air attacks that began on 24 December 1944 when the weather cleared, suffering heavy losses but inflicting critical damage on the German armour. The need for the Typhoon squadrons to be located as close to the front as possible made them very vulnerable during Operation Bodenplatte, the final major Luftwaffe operation of the war. This was meant to be a knock-out blow, in which the Luftwaffe would inflict such heavy damage on the Allied air forces as to knock them out of the fighting. The actual result was the reverse of this. Allied losses were heavy, but they could easily be replaced. The eight Typhoon squadrons then based at Eindhoven lost nineteen aircraft destroyed and fourteen damaged, mostly on the ground. Luftwaffe losses were also heavy, but could not be replaced. Operation Bodenplatte was the end of the Luftwaffe as a significant factor in the war.

This did not mean that Typhoon losses ended. The main danger to the low flying Typhoons was posed by anti-aircraft fire, not enemy aircraft. Between D-Day and the end of the war in Europe some 500 Typhoons were lost in action. During this period the rocket armed Typhoons destroyed countless German tanks, firing just under 200,000 rockets in action. The failed interceptor of 1942 had become the RAF's most effective ground attack aircraft of 1944-45.

Typhoon 1B Statistics
Production: *3,330*
Engine: *Napier Sabre IIA 24 cylinder H-form sleeve valve*
Horsepower: *2,180*
Span: *41ft 7in*
Length: *31ft 11in*
Max Speed: *412 mph*
Ceiling: *35,200ft*
Range: *980 miles with drop tanks*
Armament: *Four 20mm cannon*
Payload: *two 1,000lb bombs or eight 60lb rockets*

Aircraft

September-October 1942: *Hawker Hurricane I and Hurricane X*

September-October 1942: *Hawker Typhoon IA*

October 1942-September 1945: *Hawker Typhoon IB*

Locations

August-December 1942: *Martlesham Heath*

December 1942-January 1943: *Sawbridgworth*

January 1943: *Snailwell*

January 1943: *Sawbridgworth*

January-March 1943: *Martlesham Heath*

March 1943: *Middle Wallop*

March 1943: *Zeals*

March-April 1943: *Middle Wallop*

April 1943: *Fairlop*

April-June 1943: *Lasham*

June-July 1943: *Appledram*

July-September 1943: *New Romney*

September 1943: *Wigtown*

September-October 1943: *New Romney*

October-December 1943: *Merston*

December 1943-January 1944: *Odiham*

January 1944: *Eastchurch*

January-April 1944: *Merston*

April-June 1944: *Hurn*

June 1944: *Coulomb*

June-July 1944: *Holmsley South*

July-August 1944: *Coulombs*

August-September 1944: *Creton*

September 1944: *Amiens/Glisy*

September 1944: *Melsbroek*

September 1944-January 1945: *Eindhoven*

February 1945: *Warmwell*

April 1945: *Enschede*

April 1945: *Rheine*

April-May 1945: *Langenhagen*
January-February-April 1945: *Helmond*

www.historyofwar.org /air/units/RAF/182_wwII

This information gives us a good idea of where Eric was while writing to Frances. We can read between the lines in order to follow his meanderings. After his training at Martlesham Heath in September 1942 one can see he was constantly on the move.

182 Squadron, Normandy 1944. Eric is on the far left, front row.

The following excerpts are from *We Flew the Rocket Firing Typhoon*, published by the Royal Netherlands Royal Air Force History Unit. When 182 Squadron was formed at Martlesham Heath in the summer of 1942, Sam Calder was one of the first pilots posted to the squadron and wrote the following:

In September 1942 I was posted to 182 Squadron at Martlesham Heath near Ipswich in Suffolk. The Commanding Officer at that moment was S/L T.P. Pugh, DFC. He was an experienced Squadron Commander who had previously led 263 Squadron. This unit was equipped with twin-engined Whirlwind aircraft.

I was posted to 182 Squadron from a Hurricane OUT in Scotland and it was in Martlesham Heath that we were confronted by the Typhoon Mk-1A. There were no pilot's notes nor had anyone seen, let alone flown, this 'monster'. The Engineer Office could only help by allowing us to jack up the 'under cart' with the aircraft on a trestle. We were advised to take off on a half throttle, tail down, so the prop would not be damaged as it only had a seven-inch clearance in the tail up position. The blitz devastated grass aerodrome at Martlesham had an extension of some hundreds of yards cut out of the gorse-like shrub to give the 'Sprog' pilots a chance of getting the thing off the ground. In spite of all these precautions, many pilots fell under the spell of the sheer power (2180HP) of the 24 cylinder H-type Napier Sabre engine and gave the aircraft full throttle, which is when the incredible right-hand torque took over and they were seen disappearing in a sharp right-hand turn, at 20-30 feet, round the corner of the Administration and Sergeant's Mess building. Apart from tails dropping off and engines going unserviceable at about five to ten hours, there was nothing to worry about flying Typhoons.

At the turn of the year the Squadron was temporarily based at Sawbridgeworth and Snailwell, but on 30th January 1943 the unit returned to Martlesham at the instigation of W/C Wilkinson DSO in order to 'scoff' (drink) the excess stock of Drambuie in the mess prior to the grass airfield, where 182 originated, being taken over by the U.S.A.A.F. We drank most of it!

In March Tom Pugh organised the whole Squadron, more than twenty aircraft, to do a demonstration take-off from New Market Racecourse, a large grass area, in echelon starboard. He left me on the ground to explain in case of a major prang. There wasn't!! Fifteen out of twenty aircraft took off, wings tucked in. The last four or five were a bit ragged but that could be expected.

The exercise was meant to assist in the 'gentle' image of the Typhoon!

On 5th April 1943 the Squadron moved to Fairlop in Essex and it was during an operation from this airfield that I had some anxious moments. I was returning from a Rhubarb (RAT 18) without my No.2 who was lost while attacking trains over Northern France. Short of fuel owing to the high power settings while across the Channel, the flying control team vectored me through the London barrage and amazingly dead over Piccadilly Circus. Later in the day I drank a very thankful couple of beers in the pub which was right alongside Fairlop Airfield.

(S/L T.P. Pugh commanded 182 Squadron until 2nd August 1943. On that day he was shot down and killed by ack-ack over Dunkirk Harbour.)

In another excerpt from *We Flew the Rocket Firing Typhoon,* one of the pilots in 182 Squadron, D. Castle, narrates a funny story that appears to have been about Flt/Lt. Hutchin, especially as Eric had told Frances in a previous letter that he was thinking about buying a car. This was a story that Eric apparently did not wish to tell Frances!

It was January 1944 and the Squadron was in winter quarters, a single skin Nissan hut at Merston, near Chichester. Our favourite watering hole in Chichester was the "Nag's Head" on the eastern side of the city, which we usually visited most evenings in the week. A number of us owned a car for which we were allowed a ration of petrol in lieu of a Travel Warrant for leave purposes. One of the pilots, whom we will call Eric, owned a Singer 9 Sports Coupe and he also had a healthy thirst which he satisfied most nights, with the odd pint or two of beer in the Nag's Head. On the road to Merston was a roundabout with the usual concrete bollards indicating the direction to take. The blackout hoods fitted to car headlights allowed very little light

This Typhoon picture clearly shows the rockets on the wings.

The cockpit of the Hawker Typhoon.

through so that they were not of much help in showing the way, particularly after a pint or two.

On a particular night and on my way back to Merston, I could see as I approached the roundabout what appeared to be the rear lights of a car apparently up on the roundabout itself. Stopping my car to see what the problem was I realized, as I approached the vehicle on the roundabout, that the engine was running and the rear wheels were turning. In the driver's seat of the Singer 9 was Eric, concentrating hard on the road in front of him. Imagine his astonishment when I tapped on his side window and he saw me standing by what he thought was a moving car. It would seem that when Eric had reached the roundabout he had gone straight on, knocked down the bollard which then lodged under the differential, lifting the rear wheels off the ground allowing them to turn freely.

The invasion markings of broad black and white stripes were applied — sometimes very roughly — to all Allied invasion aircraft at the time of D-Day as a visual identification aid to hopefully avoid "friendly fire" by Allied aircraft and naval/army anti-aircraft.

Clarification courtesy Andrew Simpson, Curator, Department of Aircraft and Exhibitors, Royal Air Force Museum, Hendon, England. www.rafmuseum.org

ABOVE: Helmond 1945. Pilots of 182 Squadron chalking a message on one of the droptanks. They adopted "Jane" of the *Daily Mirror* newspaper and would often glue her strip cartoons on the tanks to send a message to the Germans.

LEFT: A Hawker Typhoon with invasion markings. Previous four photographs courtesy *We Flew the Rocket Firing Typhoon*.

CHAPTER TEN

On Active Duty

On June 6th 1944, more than 10,000 aircraft took part in the Allied landings on D-Day. In the British sector of the landing area, 12 Typhoon squadrons attacked strong points, coming in at low levels to strike beach defences, batteries, and headquarters. In the intensive immediate aftermath of the invasion, Eric's opportunities to write were sporadic at best as is made obvious in the following letters.

Tuesday, 13th June 1944

My Dearest Frances, —
For the first time I don't think I need give you any explanation for not having replied before — as you'll probably understand, we've been rather busy in the last few weeks. The squadron swing section is in the middle of a jam session at the moment so I hope you won't mind the odd mistake here and there — I'm something of a fan myself.

Tuesday, 15th

I'm afraid there'll be quite a number of interruptions like this. I just didn't see this all day yesterday and in the evening I could do nothing but fall into bed and sleep. However, for once I'm not on a show this morning so I have a little time to myself.

Now — freedom for women. (This is getting rather like an election campaign!) Surely the fact that the case you mentioned was in the newspapers suggests that it was rather unusual. Anyway, I can assure you that there is very little difference between America and England. No-one takes any notice of the old judges who have to make their own little laws — law doesn't mean very much anyway — if a thing "isn't done" — if it "isn't quite evident," one doesn't do it and everyone's happy. But let's drop the subject — these American versus England discussions never get anyone anywhere — remember the five senators? They caused more hard feelings than Goebbels ever could — and everything they said was utter rot anyway.

This is unexpected — I have the whole afternoon to myself. Maybe there'll be no more interruptions — maybe. I've bought the car — and sold it again. It was rather a wreck, but luckily I didn't lose on the deal. While I had it — for about a week — I had lots of fun playing around with the engine. I didn't find it quite so reliable as a Merlin! I've tried to — or am about to try — to draw it for you. I don't think you build this type in the

States — it's something between a convertible and a racing car — very small, very low built and <u>very</u> fast.

Sorry

H'mm. Maybe a little too long.

This one is most like it.

O. K. ?

Darling, I can't tell you how happy your letter has made me. Maybe that was all I wanted to know — that you would have said "yes" if the circumstances had been more favourable. I'm rather ashamed to admit it, but after your previous letter I had begun to doubt if you still loved me. I never could see any reason for it. I am a normally bad type, with the average little vices — and no special virtues, and the answer to that question —why you should fall in love with me — you who are so perfect in every way — has always escaped me. You know darling, I worship you. You are so wonderful and it seems so many centuries since I saw you that the memory of you is like a dream — though much more sweet and lovely than any dream could ever be. One of my greatest ambitions was to finish my first tour and then to be posted out to Falcon Field as an instructor — but I don't suppose that will happen now — I guess we'll have to wait until after the war. Till then would you do something to keep those doubts at bay? The odd reminder would be very helpful.

I'm rather worried about Ian. I wrote to him about two months ago and have had no reply yet. He is usually so much more conscientious with his mail than I am so I'm afraid he may have bought it. Anyway, I'll write to his C.O. and find out. I thought it was too good to be true — I'm on a show this evening. Briefing is at 7.30 — it's now 6.30 so I just have time. I'll try to finish this when I get back. Sorry, false alarm. The show has been put back an hour, so I can carry on. Incidentally, in case the censor is thinking of removing this, I should add that by the time this letter is posted, all the details will be very well known to the Hun, especially the results! This paper isn't really too heavy for air mail — four pages just come inside the half ounce. That reminds me — since you liked that photograph so much, I've decided to send you a smaller version of it — one small enough for you to carry around with you — I don't intend giving you any chance of forgetting me!

I was surprised to hear Dibble was married. Remember New Year's Eve — when Ian and I both stayed in Phoenix? I still kick myself for letting you sleep on that sofa. Anyway Dibble was our alibi — he took us both into Mesa and we went straight to Phoenix — claiming next morning that we did not know we had to return. He backed us too — quite a good type.

So you like strings. In that case, I have just the thing for you. It is "Tales from the Vienna Woods" — the recording is by the Philadelphia Symphony conducted by Leopold Stokowski. It's the best waltz recording I've ever heard — and I think it will convince your brother that strings are anything but shallow. I'm afraid we are to be interrupted again — the show was rescheduled after all, but I have to be up at 3:30 am so I must get some sleep. Goodnight, darling.

I believe today is 27th but it may be 26th or the 28th — I've lost count. I've been fighting a losing battle ever since D-Day. I owe a dozen or so letters to various people and there seems to be very little hope of ever writing them all. However life is much less monotonous these days — I've been having a lot of fun with the doodle bugs. The things look very weird from the ground — it's a queer sensation — watching one fly past through the most terrific flak, knowing that there's no-one in it — and praying that it won't be shot down until it has passed overhead! As you know, they are a piece of cake to us — no return fire, no evasive action — it's almost too easy.

I hope you don't think I forgot your birthday — I was thinking of it a month before, but I was on the very edge of the world at the time and I couldn't get to a cable office. However, I'll send a cable just as soon as I can, even if it is rather late.

You will probably receive a letter from Dave Maugy soon — he has some wonderful scheme all worked out to speed up our mails. Unluckily I've completely forgotten how he intends to do it so I'll leave it to him to explain. Dave is a Lieutenant in the U.S.A.A.F over here — I met him some time ago in my travels when we were at the same station together. He's an extremely good type — visits our squadron whenever he has time — in fact he has been trying to get himself attached to us as an American liaison officer. I believe he's rather rolling in dollars back home — spends his time lounging around Miami Beach. Actually he advised me on your birthday present — so don't blame me!

*I'm afraid I must finish this off darling, otherwise it will never be posted. On reading it over it seems horribly disconnected — but I suppose that's understandable. Bung ho child, remember me to the family,
All my love, Eric*

P.S. I couldn't be quite sure from that photograph of course, but I gather that little Frances is getting to be quite a big girl now. How does it feel to be nineteen? Ho hum! Wish I was young again!

On June 22, 1944, the squadron was brought back to Detling in Kent to help counter the menace of the V-1 attacks on London and the Home Counties. The V-1 was an unmanned, unguided, flying bomb, essentially the first cruise missile. Designed for the terror bombing of London, it was called *Vergeltungswaffe* or "retaliation weapon" by the Germans but derided as the Buzz Bomb or Doodlebug by the English. It was basically a liquid fuelled, pulse-jet drone aircraft that could carry a 2,000-pound warhead. There was no navigation system, so it was just pointed in the direction of its target. Simple gyrocompasses kept it level, and range was controlled by the fuel supply.

The first V-1 offensive had been launched on June 12, prompted by the successful Allied landing in Europe on D-Day, June 6. Once the Germans got their stride they launched an average of 190 V-1 rockets a day, but the British quickly became adept at spotting and shooting them down and only about 25 percent of the V-1s hit their target. Still, a total of 9,521 V-1s were fired at southeast England, causing 22,892 casualties, almost entirely civilians. The first line of defense against them were the fighters (Mosquitoes, Spitfires and Typhoons) piloted by Eric and his comrades, who flew to intercept them. Six days after his squadron took up this duty, at precisely 18.30 hours on June 28, while patrolling in a Spitfire at 2,000 feet over the Canterbury Isle of Sheppy sector, Eric encountered and shot down his first Doodlebug.

As Axis troops were withdrawn, the squadron returned to the European mainland, flying everywhere over the front. Because the airstrips were often only a few miles behind the frontlines, the ground crew could see the squadron aircraft take off, climb, and attack the enemy troop concentrations and strong points. According to one pilot they would just take off, wind up to 7,000 feet behind the lines, then go down on the target and be back in 20 minutes having fired their rockets. They would then rearm, refuel, and away they went again.

Now that the D-Day push was over Eric was at liberty to give Frances more information about the missions he had been flying.

Friday 22nd September '44

My Dearest Frances,

I must apologise (again!) for not writing before. I just don't seem to be able to settle down to anything these days — and anyway I've always been a totally bad correspondent. My letters seem to consist of nothing but apologies for something or other — I must be a very bad type.

I have some very promising news of Ian. It seems he was shot up by flak just before D-Day and made a successful forced landing somewhere on the Cherbourg peninsula. After he landed he told the boys over the R.T. that he was o.k., so I imagine he is now a prisoner.

So little Frances is going to the Big, Bad City — I imagine she's feeling quite grown up! I wonder if I should give her some advice — but I don't think she needs it — I'm quite sure it's impossible for her to be a bad girl! (I hope you don't take that as a challenge!) While you are there, though, you really must see the "Ice Follies" at the PanPacific Stadium on Beverly Boulevard — it's terrific. I can also recommend Earl Carrol — though, as I said before, he missed one. (I hope I did say that before!) Places I would not recommend are the Florentine Gardens (!!), the "Jade" night-club (where my jacket was picked — remember?), and the "Streets of Paris" just opposite the "Jade" — one of the lowest joints in town. All of the last three are on Hollywood Boulevard. By the way, if you'd like to try a screen version of English food try "St. Donats" at 8351 Sunset Boulevard. You remember Mrs. Day? Why not go to see her — I'm sure you would be very welcome and you would love her — she's one of the most wonderful people I've ever met. Of course, I have an ulterior motive — she's an absolutely wonderful cook, and, while I admit I've never tried yours, I imagine she could give you a lot of useful hints! Anyway, she always welcomed new recruits to the ranks of her hostesses — she runs a sort of miniature D.W.R. of her own, you know. Incidentally,

I believe her daughter Shirley is at Pomona College. Don't ask her too many questions about me though, you might hear something you shouldn't know! Mrs. Day's address is: 2049 Oakstone Way, Laurel Canyon Road, Hollywood. Laurel Canyon Road crosses the top of Hollywood Boulevard and Oakstone Way is a turning of it.

This letter seems to developing into a guide to L.A. — though you probably know more about the place than I do. The last time I saw Claremont was in November '42 — Ian and I had left L.A. at sunset and hit Claremont at around 11:00 pm — we had been delayed by a type who insisted on buying us a drink. About all I remember of the place was a little drug store on a corner where we had a sandwich and I did my best to console the young wolf — he had just left Marilyn! Afterwards it took us an hour to thumb a ride and we both agreed we never wanted to see Claremont again. I must admit my views have changed since then — right now I can't think of a better place to be.

There is really no reason now why you shouldn't know something of what I've been doing since I got back to England. It's all history now, so the censor won't mind (I hope!) I hope you don't think I want to shoot a line — it's just that you've asked me many times to tell you where I am and what I'm doing. As you'll have gathered from the post-marks on my letters I've been around quite a bit — in fact in the last two years I've seldom stayed in one place more than two weeks. I first joined

an operational squadron in November of last year —
flying Typhoons. After a spot of dive bombing, escorting
etc, I got my wish and went on to Spitfires — the best
little aeroplane in the world. We had a lot of fun train
busting, dive bombing, escorting and doing a lot of
shows at low level shooting of anything military-look-
ing. While we were doing this my aircraft was hit on
one show — luckily it was nothing serious. After D-Day
we did the odd beach-head patrol — without, however,
seeing the Luftwaffe — and then I went on doodle-bug-
ging — a lot of fun at first but it got very boring towards the end. I wasn't on that for very long, however,
though it was long enough to be shot up by flak again
— friendly stuff this time, and more serious — it burst a
tyre and wrecked my engine — which finally cut on me
just as I was landing. Seven American P38's mistook me
for a Hun once and tried to shoot me down. They didn't
make it — but they succeeded in scaring me quite a bit.
At the moment I'm flying Typhoons again and waiting
to go to France (or Belgium) to shoot rockets at tanks
— which should be quite good fun.

On reading that over it sounds like a horrible line,
but I'll leave it in — you may find it interesting. I'm
afraid I've rather neglected this letter this evening —
you'll see why when you receive the parcel which will
start on its way at the same time as this letter. I believe I've already disclaimed all responsibility for the
contents of the parcel. It all started way back in May
when Ian was on leave. My mother — jokingly at first —
made the suggestion. I was definitely not in favour at

first. I thought it was not exactly the sort of thing one sent to one's girlfriend — too — well you know what I mean (or at least you will when the parcel arrives!) Dave persuaded me that it would be o.k., and I was finally talked into it — mainly, I must admit, because I couldn't make any other suggestions! Now it's ready for mailing, but I'll leave you to guess what it is. It's the sadist in me that builds up your curiosity like this!

At the moment I'm living in a tent — not a bad life when one gets used to it, but it's rather hard to write letters, as I trust you'll excuse any depreciation in my scribbling, if that is possible.

I'm afraid I must finish now and write a short note to pop in the parcel. Goodnight, darling.

All my love, Eric

Saturday, 23rd September, '44

Darling, At last — here it is. It will be nearer to Christmas than your birthday, I'm afraid, but I believe my mother had some trouble finding wool. In case you haven't gathered what it is — my mother describes it as "the sort of thing one wears when one is having break-fast in bed". I presume that means anytime one is feel-ing lazy and prefers bed to any other place. (If you are like me, that is just about any time.) Anyway, now you see what I mean. My mother, of course, made it - she

spends all her spare time knitting — but don't tell anyone — I had a hand in it too. While I admit it's not the
sort of thing one expects an R.A.F. pilot to do, I had to
put something towards it — so I — er — I put the wings
on. I'm rather proud of my first attempt at embroidery
— though I imagine your rather more expert eye will
find it rather amateurish. Anyway, I hope you like it —
and please spare my blushes! I'm also enclosing my old
squadron badge — it's part of the coat of arms of the
squadron — which, is, of course, No. 1 — or the "Fightin'
Foist Pursoot", as Dave calls it. It is the oldest squadron
in the R.AF. — way back in 1911 we had balloons and
bikes! I must away to bed — it's 12:45 am.

> All my love, darling,
> Eric

P.S. Thanks for the wizard card — it boosted my morale
no end. Incidentally, it got here in thirteen days —
not bad.
P.P.S. I'm afraid the Post Office have been having trouble
with your "fours" again. Yours is like this:- 4. They seem
to think it should look like this:- **4**. These are forgeries of
yours and theirs, by the way — a little hobby of mine.

Come sa, m'selle 4, pas comme ça **4**. Cela est comme un (or une) seven.

Excuse the wrappings - they were the best I could do.

CHAPTER ELEVEN
Life in Holland

By the autumn of 1944 Eric was stationed in Holland and the war seemed to be winding down somewhat, maybe the beginning of the end. With the holidays approaching Eric was starting to think about Christmas 1942 and the heady few days he spent with Frances during that time. Sometimes his nerves seemed a little on edge, not surprising considering the life he was leading, dicing with death on a daily basis. Many of his Royal Air Force friends had been shot down and killed; his living conditions were primitive and he never knew where he would be from one day to the next. Yet somehow he managed to keep his sense of humour and his love for Frances carried him through those dark and troubled days.

182 Squadron, R.A.F.

31st October, '44

My Dearest Frances,
I'm afraid this will be rather short — air letters don't allow much space for the usual eight pages effort. However, I believe they have priority over normal air mail, so you would get this in about two weeks. You know, you are a little girl of many parts. Is that a rather surprising statement? But you surprise me even more. All this — and an authority of juvenile delinquency too — of all things!! Frankly you amaze me! Yes, I've learned

your guilty secret. It gave me about the biggest shock I've ever had in my life — of all places, a tent on an airfield in Holland was the last place I expected to find a photograph of you. Your fame has spread through a very old back number of the Saturday Evening Post. "Surely I've seen that blonde somewhere before" — going through all the blondes I've ever known — a lengthy process of course! — and then comparing her with the one that sits beside my bed — er figuratively of course! Actually that's not how it happened at all. I always look through "Life" etc., with the idea at the back of my mind that someday I'll find you there, and when I turned the page that photograph just jumped out and hit me. I was literally dazed for some time, and when I finally recovered I was like a dog with two tails — or a man in love with a new photograph! I'm afraid the lights have gone out and writing by the light of candle isn't too good for the old peepers, so I'll pack in until tomorrow,

Goodnight darling,

Eric

I hope you like the whatsit I sent — even though it was a little late. I had an awful feeing of finality after it was posted, but I suppose I'll find I needn't have worried anyway, I hope! I'm afraid this letter is very disconnected — it was hard enough to concentrate on writing any sort of sense when I was in England — out here in Holland it's next to impossible. There are so many things to think about, conditions are rather primitive and life is even more uncertain than it was in England. At least the shows in those days were fairly stereotypical — almost monotonously so in fact. But now one never knows where we will be or what one will be doing next. It adds a certain spice to the work, of course, and it's a lot of fun seeing Europe at the expense of a magnanimous government, but it's wearing on the nerves, and for the first time in my life I find myself dreaming of and almost imagining a little peace and quiet and that secure sense of exactly where you'll be next week. Unfortunately I also know quite well that I'd be bored to tears after the first couple of weeks. We have quite a lot of fun out here — you've no idea how amusing it is to hold a conversation with someone who knows as little of your language as you know of his — precisely nothing. Actually it's amazing how easy it is to say what one wants to say by means of a few gestures and similar sounding words. Of course, there are misunderstandings which are usually amusing but sometimes embarrassing! There, I'm afraid I must leave you. Write soon please, darling,

        Always yours, Eric

P.S. Write to this address — normal air mail with a ten cent stamp — but consult the Post Office first!

182 Squadron, R.A.F.

Sunday, 3rd December '44

My Dearest Frances,

After long consideration I've decided to start off with some bad news and get it over. No it's not about me — my luck has held so far — apart from the odd hole in a wing or tail plane. I'm sorry if I've raised your hopes for Ian's safety — though I believe I said I couldn't promise anything. I am in his old squadron now, and word came through a few days ago that he had been killed in action. There were no details — just the bare statement. You know how I feel about it, so I won't make any comment — and anyway the last thing I can afford to do is to start getting sentimental over these things — the day that happens is the day I put in for a rest. I hope you won't think I'm being callous by writing a normal letter — I know how hard it must be for you to understand how I can write a normal letter after this, but I am sure you will realize that if one remained morbid for very long every time a chap bought it, however close a friend he happened to be, then it would not be very long before one's nerve cracked — and that happens soon enough anyway. The only way is to say "Well, he was a grand fellow, but he just isn't around any more" — and then just forget it. The day the news came through there were just four of us left on the squadron who remembered him. Now there are only two... so you see it wouldn't be very good for our own little war effort if we just sat around thinking about it.

We had a big party at our mess last night — the first of the Christmas series. Yesterday, incidentally, was December 6th — I'm afraid this letter has been neglected for some time — anyway December 6th is St. Nicholas Day in Holland — a sort of children's Christmas day. The R.A.F. of course, with their usual enthusiasm for local customs (see hay rides, hot dog picnics, etc.), seized on the idea as an excuse to throw an extra Christmas party. Other fascinating, though not quite as local, customs were indulged inasmuch as the drinking of liberal quantities of champagne — with the result that a number of pasty-faced and sour looking officers sat down to breakfast at a late hour this morning — luckily the weather was too bad for flying. Actually it was quite a good party — our mess was once a convent, but I'm sure the nuns would never have recognized the place. Hmmm, I wonder if this will tempt you to give me a lecture on the evils of demon alcohol. You have, no doubt, noticed that my writing is wandering all over the page even more vaguely than usual — purely the result of lack of sleep, I assure you! Which reminds me, there's a very comfortable looking bed just behind me — and I last saw it in the wee small hours this morning — and I feel myself quite unable to control my pen any longer — and I'm feeling d'li'fly drowsy — and in fact, I'm going to bed.

Goodnight darling. Eric

Friday 8th

I feel much better today — I can think of the party without having to take a preparatory aspirin first. I can even see what I'm writing — and on looking over page two I find it wasn't as wavy as it looked last night — I must have been writing on instruments. Talking of instruments, how is dear old Falcon getting along these days? Of course I realise the general tone of the place must have lowered considerably when the star course left, but I suppose the odd bod does stagger into the air occasionally without too disastrous results. You haven't mentioned the Field, the cadets, or the British War Relief for some time. I hope they are all still operational.

You know, this is the longest letter I've written since I've been here. I'm rather enjoying it — apart from the fact that I can't think of very much to say and anyway it seems to be taking rather a long time to say that. I suppose there are lots of little things I could tell you about Holland which you would find very interesting, but they are all so commonplace to me that I can't sort out those which are worth talking about. (Something about not being able to see wood for trees would be appropriate there.) However, I'll try to find a few clips for you.

The Dutch are quite nice types, though they appear to be rather dim at times. They are the most unemotional people I've ever come in contact with — Americans consider Englishmen rather reserved, but I can assure you we have nothing on these stolid Dutchmen. The only time I've ever seen them give vent to their feelings was when we paid a short (very short!) visit to the front line one day and gave the army a hand in liberating a town. Then they really let their hair down — especially when they saw the R.A.F. markings on our truck. I never realised the R.A.F. were so popular. However, when we went back there a few days later they were just the same as ever. I'm afraid there's not much fun to be had in these Dutch towns — most of our amusement is provided by ourselves — that is by E.N.S.A., which is the British equivalent of the U.S. Special Service Division. Actually, most of the shows are extremely good — usually straight from London with the original cast, while the films are those which are currently running in England. One of our favourite means of enjoying ourselves is to organise a trip up to the front line to have a look at the war on the ground. From what I've seen of it so far, I'm darned glad I'm in the R.A.F. — even though the army boys say just the opposite — "You wouldn't get me in one of those infernal machines for all the tea in China" is a typical remark. The idea behind these trips is to pick up souvenirs in the shape of Nazi flags and notices, cans, guns etc. The most prized piece of booty, loot or what you will, is a German automatic — either a Luger or a Mauser, they are, to us the most beautiful pieces of work in the gun world. Unluckily, however, they are not too plentiful — one must get there before the army, and wandering around in no-man's land is not too healthy a pastime — it arouses the ire of both our own brass hats and of the dreaded Hun. On one *occasion we had a look at a concentration camp — a horrible place. It used to be known to the Dutch as the "hygienic hell" — it has been left scrupulously clean and bare. There was an atmosphere and a silence about the place which I can only describe, rather melodramatically, I'm afraid, as an atmosphere of death. The noise of bursting shells was, of course, just as loud inside the gates as outside, but somehow it didn't seem to penetrate, as if one had a wet blanket covering the whole camp. As we drove in it was like entering a different world and everyone instinctively started to talk in whispers. One of the strangest things was the complete lack of birds, although there were flocks of them chirping in the trees outside there wasn't one inside the barbed wire. As you can imagine we were very glad to get out again.*

I wish my writing didn't have this annoying habit of sloping up towards the right hand side of the page —I don't seem to be able to do anything to stop it. However, you never seem to have any trouble reading my letters, so I guess it doesn't matter.

I'm sorry, I've tried hard, but I'm afraid I must admit failure — I just can't think of anything more to say — this letter has taken too long to write anyway. So — buenas noches, hasta la vista. And all that.

> *All my love darling,*
> *Eric*

P.S. what is the opinion of the Pomona girls of your R.A.F. boyfriend? (I'm afraid that's rather ambiguous — I mean, of course, theirs of me).

182 Squadron, R.A.F. c/o B.L.A.*

Le 22 Decembre, 1944

Cherie, J'ai retourné judgement de Bruxelles ou j'ai trouvé que je parle la language Français mieux que j'en ouffsé. Or maybe you don't think so. Anyway, considering that I haven't looked at, heard or spoken French for five years I got along far better than I had expected in the admittedly rather ungrammatical remains of my schoolboy French. Towards the end of my stay there I found I could understand just what people were saying and I was even thinking in French. Incidentally I've found one error in my above attempt — it should be Je vien de retourné de Bruxelles — but let's drop the subject.

Brussels is a wizard city — just the perfect place to spend a couple of days leave. I found the pace a little hard however, on both my pocket and myself! I found some Chanel perfume for you, by the way, it's not number five I'm afraid but it has the same effect, so I suggest

---

* B.L.A. stands for British Liberation Army. During 1945 the B.L.A. liberated great parts of Holland from German occupation. Eric received his mail in care of them.

you exercise some caution in using it — a small dab would be useful protection, though I don't suppose even that would hold back all the wolves. Even the R.A.F, hardened and cynical though they may be, have been known to stagger slightly and develop a somewhat glazed look about the eyes when the full force of Monsieur Chanel's blitzkrieg has been turned on them. I'm writing this in dispersal and some of the boys are waving bottles of various perfumes around — it creates a wizard atmosphere — though I can't tell you how they described it!

This is the second attempt at writing to you that I've made in the last few days. The first time I was feeling rather elated after landing from a particularly interesting show, with the result that I shot two pages of the most awful lines ever — and then decided that it was all censorable and would end up as Exhibit A in a court-martial if any censor got hold of it. It read rather like a really sensational newspaper report and would probably have given you the impression that I had turned into a callous and indiscriminate killer which actually may not be very far from the truth. (!)

Have you any photographs knocking around which feel capable of making the trip across the Atlantic — I'd like to see how you look now you're a big girl.

It's very encouraging to find you like fog, rain, cold etc. — though I can assure you that if you were in my position you would be as heartily sick of all three as

I am. However, I should train you for England...or is that subject forbidden?

I found the episode of the escalator very amazing — I hadn't realized you had never seen the things before. As you probably know, London is just honeycombed with an underground train system, and all the stations are a maze of subways and escalators. I can't even remember the first time I used one, don't suppose I could even walk at the time.

Another letter from you arrived last night — the second in a week. I'll have to do more of this letter writing, y'know — I never realized before what a help it would be to my morale. And the photograph — unguarded moment or not, darling it's absolutely wizard — you seem to get more beautiful every day. I wish I had more room on this thing to tell you more, but I promise I'll write another long letter tonight — and I'll try to finish it a little quicker this time too — the last one took me nearly a week! I really must close now — see you tonight darling,

All my love, Eric;

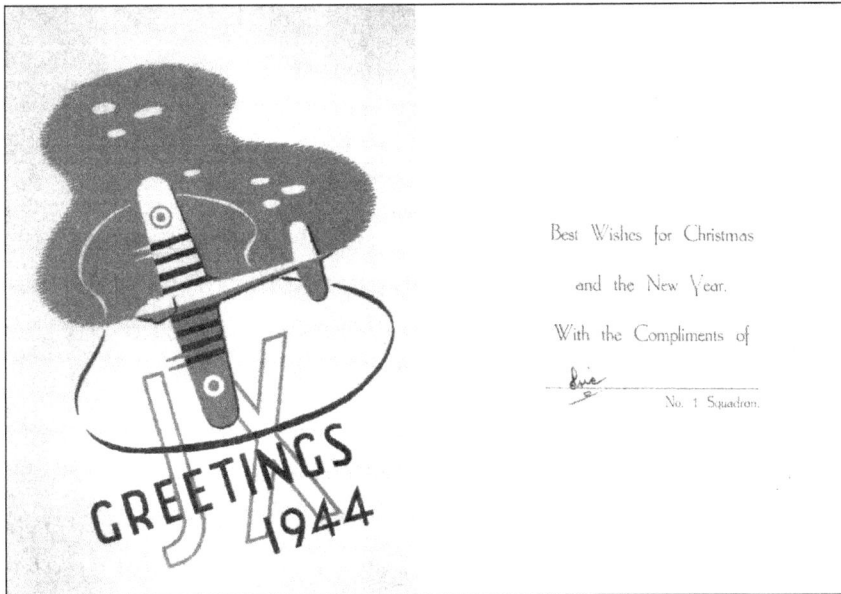

Best Wishes for Christmas

and the New Year.

With the Compliments of

No. 1 Squadron.

GREETINGS 1944

Note inside the
1944 Christmas Card

182 Squadron R.A.F.

24th December 1944

Dearest Frances,

Christmas Eve. There's a terrific party going on down-
stairs — I've been there for three hours or so — drinking, I'm afraid, but I just can't seem to work up any interest in it at all. There seems to be something lacking
— it's you of course, somehow you and Christmas seem
to be tied up — it just isn't complete without you. Incidentally, while I'm in this mood I must apologize for
that air letter I sent you a few weeks ago — I'm afraid
it wasn't very cheerful, but that's the way I think when
I'm feeling low.

The party has just broken up — somebody is wishing
everybody else a Merry Christmas, and a lot of rather
drunken types have just staggered into my room, apparently with the objective of distracting my attention
from this letter. Actually, I'm a little bit that way myself — bad show and all that — but there isn't anything
else to do in this — bland country. But I must dash off
to bed — I believe I'm on the early show in the morning
and I must get some sleep.

Goodnight darling, Eric

.

I'm afraid this letter has been neglected for far too
long — it's now one o'clock in the morning of January 3rd. It was unavoidable however — I had to come
to England one day and couldn't get back for nearly

a week. When I did return it was time for me to come home again on a weeks leave — so here I am — I always seem to be home for the New Year. For the first time since I've been in the R.A.F. I really feel I need this break. Usually I spend the first four days in bed and then become bored and impatient to get back. Recently however, the pace has been getting a little hot, and though I never thought I would reach this stage, I am beginning to look forward to my six months rest, which is due to start in June. Even so, I know that after the first few quiet weeks of a reasonably safe life on some peaceful training station, I'll just be counting the days to getting back on a squadron again — but that's how it is —this life just gets to you, and though sooner or later it must be your turn you can't stay away from it. I only hope the war will be over before I find myself saying "this is it". I seem to have slipped into a most morbid subject, especially in that last bit. It's a bad thing to tempt fate like that.

Thanks a lot for writing to my mother darling, she asked me several times what you thought of the "whatsit" and she was delighted when you wrote to her yourself — though I'm having some trouble in telling her exactly what she must not say about me when she writes to you — in fact it's almost amounting to blackmail! Since she refuses to allow me to either dictate or censor the letter I can only say that I deny everything — and anyway she doesn't really know what her little son does when she is not around to keep him in check. Anyway, I plead "not guilty" and I trust the judge will exercise extreme leniency in passing sentence — the jury's verdict is a foregone conclusion in face of the conclusive evidence which will no doubt be produced by the learned counsel for the prosecution. Hmmm. Maybe I should have been a lawyer. Anyway, I am glad you like the — er — thingummy (what is that thing called anyway?).

I must admit I breathed a sigh of relief when I found I'd got away with it. It's rather wonderful to know you've been "thrilled beyond words" with everything I've given you. You don't have to thank me, you know, darling — the knowledge that I've done something to make you happy is enough. And anyway, how does it go? ... and with all my worldly goods I thee endow. Everything I have is yours, and all that ... but we're getting into a dangerous subject — or don't you recognize the quotation. If you don't I won't enlighten you — I hope you'll hear me say it all one day ... perhaps I shouldn't have said that, but after all, you can't stop me dreaming.

Darling, it's half past two — I really must go to bed.
      Bonsoir, Eric

That's twice I've signed this letter — I'll finish it tonight even if it means I don't go to bed at all.

You know you'll find ice skating easier than roller skating — it's almost impossible to fall backward. I dabble in it occasionally myself, and speaking from experience I would advise you to choose a time when the ice is dry for your first attempt! Talking of the roller skating episode — that was a classic! — did Ian and I act as little gentlemen should? I can't quite remember but I expect we were rather amused!

I was very glad to hear that Claude had received his commission. If he ever gets to come over here you must give him my address and I'll show him the Big City — at least you'll be able to keep a close check on me!

I was rather surprised at your views on the bombing of Tokyo — I don't understand how you feel any pity for any Jap soldier or civilian. Remember that they are the same people who are daily torturing American and British prisoners. One cannot consider them in the same light as one would consider normal human beings. They are just particularly vicious animals which must be wiped out. Beside the Japs even the Huns seem more than playful kittens — and that is certainly not the way they appear to the peoples of the occupied European countries. Presumably if you feel pity for the people of Tokyo you must feel even more for those same people of Berlin, Cologne, Hamburg etc. yet these are the people who in the last seventy years have three times brought more misery and suffering to Europe than all the wars of civilization has ever known. To give one instance, in that concentration camp I visited, before the Huns pulled out they shot, hung and burned alive every one of the 13,000 prisoners. Supposing you were behind a bomb sight of one of those B-29's and you knew you were bombing people who were worse than this, would you feel any pity or remorse? This reads too much like a propaganda leaflet — I'd better stop before my pen runs away with me.

You ask me how I like the Dutch girls. That is rather a sore point with us — there seem to be very few left at all, those one does see are mostly between five and fifteen or fifty and a hundred. And of those who are a reasonable age I have yet to find one who could be called beautiful by any standards. No, you have nothing to fear from the Dutch girls — but the Belgian girls — aha!! They really have something — it's hard to find one who doesn't resemble an angel — and the quantity, as well as the quality is quite terrific. The most amazing contrast to the Dutch people, however, is in their temperament — here are two countries whose total territory could be lost between Phoenix and Tucson and yet one is calm and reserved while the other is gay, excitable and almost embarrassingly friendly (I shall never forget seeing a purple British army sergeant being kissed on both cheeks by an excited little Belgian man!) Their one aim in life seems to be to squeeze as much fun out of it as possible — and they certainly seem to succeed. However, I can assure you that all the gorgeous beauties of Brussels pale into insignificance beside you, my darling — or does that sound like a line?

I got the gen on the addressing and stamping of your letters from one of the boys who has a girlfriend in Pasadena, but I have since gathered that she used a special air mail service which goes by air only across America and by sea across the Atlantic. Anyway I guess the Post Office knows best. Now I must close for the third time!

Sweet dreams, all my love, Eric

P.S. What did — or what will your mother say when she found or finds what I gave you for your birthday? Was she shocked? (Or will she be?)

P.P.S. The word "gotten" is never used in England, so my grammar isn't exactly as bad as it appears on page 3. I believe it is an old English word which went to America with the Pilgrim Fathers and then went out of usage over here. Hmm, that's a point too — use or usage. I'm afraid my brain is too dull at this late hour to decide.

On New Year's Day 1945, any hopes of a lie-in following the previous nights' New Year's Eve festivities were well and truly scuppered by a surprise early-morning German aircraft bombing and strafing attack that lasted 20 minutes and left the squadron with not one serviceable aircraft. Other squadrons received similar battering from some 400 German aircraft, which proved to be the Luftwaffe's last action, after which they were never again a threat.

It was then on to Helmond, the Netherlands, later that same month and then back to England for rocket training at Wormwell, Dorset, in February 1945, then back again across the North Sea to Helmond and finally to Enschede, the Netherlands in April 1945.

Flight Lieutenant E. G. Hutchin
182 Squadron, R.A.F.

Undated letter, probably around March 1945

My Dearest Frances,
What shall I say? I can only tender my most abject apologies and trust that you will forgive me. It's — let me see — must be nearly two months since I last wrote to you — I've received ("e" or "i" first) three letters and quite a batch of photographs from you in that time — and today you thanked me for all my letters — a real stab in the back for my conscience! Seriously though, darling, I really am ashamed of myself — it only helps to prove what a bad type I am (y'know if I go on telling you that you will begin to believe it!) Anyway, am I forgiven? To show you that my mind is sometimes capable of reaching a somewhat higher plane than usual here are a few verses written by a R.C.A.F. pilot which I think

are rather fine. They may give you a small idea of how a pilot feels when he flies for the fun of it — he calls it "High Flight" — I would prefer the title to be "Ode to a Spitfire" — something equally fatuous ... I think it would be as well if we put it all on the next page — it will look better — so would you — mind — just — turning — over — ? Thank you. Here we go —

Oh, I have slipped the surly bonds of earth
And danced the skies on laughter-silvered wings.
Onward I've climbed, and joined the tumbling mirth
Of sun-split clouds - and done a hundred things
You have not dreamed of - wheeled and soared and swung
High in the sunlit silence; hov'ring there,
I've chased the shouting wind along, and flung
My eager craft through footless halls of air.
Up, up the long, delirious, burning blue
I've topped the wind-swept heights with easy grace
Where never lark, or even eagle flew -
And, while with silent lifting mind I've trod
The high untrespassed sanctity of space,
Put out my hand and touched the face of God.

This is a complete answer to the question people who've never flown always ask me — "What's it like flying up there all alone?" I don't think I've ever seen it expressed so well before — flying is the hardest thing to put into words — but this chap has done it perfectly. Feel you'd like to fly? I'll take you up sometime.

Before I go any further, and in case you haven't noticed it already, I must call your attention to my new rank — top right hand corner of page 1, bottom left hand corner of the front of the envelope and the top of the back of the envelope — Flight Lieutenant, Flight Looie, Flight Loot, F/Lt., or what you will — you darling, as a very special favour may call me Captain — but please, not on the envelope! Anyway, the only thing which interests me is the pay — now around the $2000 a year mark — you see I'm very mercenary too!

You suggest that I may feel rather more than two years older than I was in '44. Hmmm. To put it mildly, you can say that again! Two years of living in close proximity to the grim reaper has aged me considerably. Ian is not the only one, you know — if I go back to the fall of '43 I can name literally scores of my close personal friends who have since been shot down — and we still read newspaper reports of Isolationist American senators making such remarks as "The British will fight to the last American." "In the north the British are marking time while the Americans do all the fighting" and so on — doesn't help to improve Anglo-American relations. Sorry darling, I'm duty pilot and my truck has just arrived so I must away to work — at the ghastly hour of 11:00 pm — and I have to be up at 6:30 am! Ugh!

This should turn out to be a very long letter — from your last three epistles I've drawn up a formidable list of things to write about and comment on and questions to answer — I've found that to be an easy way to write a letter without getting stuck for something to talk about. Add to that the odd impromptu paragraphs which seem to flow out of my pen without any conscious guidance from me — such as the above bind about isolationist senators — one of my pet aversions — and we shall have at least eight pages. First on the list is the word "photographs" — which subject will probably end by my getting lyrical about such things as your eyes, your hair, and the squadron pin, which has never appeared in a more lovely setting. Tell me, darling, how come you're so cute? Each succeeding photograph shows you more beautiful than the last, and in this last one, while you still retain that wide-eyed, innocent, out-of-this-world look, you seem to have added a touch of glamour — which has proved very effective — you have the whole of 182 squadron at your feet!

My room is now more than ever a rendezvous for the boys — they all come and gaze admiringly at your photographs — though they show the most unflattering surprise that an old reprobate like myself should even move in the same world as such a divine angel. I now have quite a collection of smaller photographs of you — in fact I'm thinking of starting an album of them — though of course it wouldn't be complete without those pictures of Baby Frances which your mother once showed me! By the way, you mentioned "very interesting comments" on my photographs by the Pomona girls. Am I allowed to ask you what the comments were? And why am I "unusual"? You've roused my curiosity, surely you won't hold out on me now!

About drink. My description of the parties was designed to obtain your views on the subject, and I'm glad they haven't changed — even though I disagree with them. The trouble is, of course, that drinking in America and drinking in England are two entirely different things. With the American — if you'll forgive me saying so — it's a case of all or nothing at all. Assuming that he drinks, he will decide to go out on a big two-day session — with the one idea of getting pie-eyed and staying that way for as long as possible. When he comes round on a Monday morning he hasn't a clue what's happened over the weekend (when he gets over the after effects) and he's quite sober for weeks afterwards — till the next time. He drinks whiskey. Englishman, on the other hand, drinks beer — large pints of it — because he likes it and because he likes to prop up the bar in the little pub around the corner and natter with his cronies over a couple of jugs of foaming ale. Occasionally he does have a party and gets mildly and pleasantly tight. Personally I love the stuff, but only in small quantities, in good company and in pleasant surroundings. The English pub is an institution much the same as the American drug store — you pop into the Owl on Main Street for a quiet coke with Margie, I pop into the "Golden Lion" in the Market Square with Joe for a quiet noggin. I drink, you don't, but I've tried both and I can assure you there's very little difference between the coke in the drug store and the odd beer in the pub. It certainly does no harm — in fact it's rather good for us — contains an enzyme called riboflavin — er, maybe it's a vitamin.

By the way, the grim reaper took a swing at me today. While he didn't quite win, his scythe only made a small hole in my tail. It was my own fault anyway. I'll be more careful in future. At least I can claim a number of flak shells destroyed. Hope the censor passes this!

I'm afraid I'm having a little trouble with the Customs and Excise over Johnny Chanel's product — it appears the R.A.F. postal types haven't taken into consideration pilots with girl-friends in the States. However, I hope to get it all sorted out soon and you'll be able to test the efficiency of your hat pin — though I don't hold any great hopes for it — I'm quite sure it wouldn't discourage a really determined wolf — such as myself — I would suggest a really good chaperone — though not an escort — not till I'm around anyway. I wasn't surprised to hear you didn't enjoy Earl Carroll's show very much — after all, it's definitely made for men. However, you seem to have been quite impressed by the sets and general staging of the thing, so presumably my reputation as a guide to Hollywood is still intact — at least my list of things to see and do appears to have met with your approval. There are of course, other places I could suggest — such as "The Streets of Paris," the "Blue Palm," and "The Jade," where I had my pocket picked. All of them were favourite haunts of Ten Course, but are hardly the sort of places where nice little girls should be seen — not if they want to stay nice little girls, anyway!

You know, I wish I could tell you more about the sort of life I lead — trouble is, it's all so bound up with flying — in fact almost my every action is governed by operations — the place I sleep, the time I get up, the food I eat (and drink!), and, of course, everything I do in the hours of daylight is directly connected with flying. Since I'm not allowed to write about Service subjects I'm not left with very much to describe! However, I may tell you that by far the greater part of my time is spent sitting around just waiting for something to happen! The fact that it usually does happen doesn't help to relieve the boredom of the waiting. Occasionally we do indulge in more strenuous forms of activity. Such as digging foxholes or swinging compasses, but we tend to get into rather a rut just sitting by the fire all day. Actually there's no reason why I shouldn't describe a show as you would see it. Dozens of people have published the same sort of thing before and since I do the odd spot of censoring myself I don't think it will give any information to the Hun.

It starts with everyone sitting around as usual. The telephone rings — 'Hello — yes — O.K. — cheerio." "Right ho chaps, briefing" — and a number of bods don coats and hats, and disappear, leaving the rest of the boys to fight over their vacated chairs by the fire. Life goes on for a time as usual, then the door opens and they all dash in — always in a terrific flap — "Where are you going?" "Oh the usual milk run to —." "Who's got my helmet?" — "Buster you go out on my right" — and so on. Then suddenly the hut is quiet again. Five minutes later you can't hear yourself think as they all start up and taxi out to take off. You settle down to a book or a letter to wait for them to come back — it may be anything from half an hour or two and a half hours. When they are due to return you find yourself listening for their engines, and when they are heard everyone scrambles for the door to count the number in the very pretty display formation beating up the aerodrome. A short interval while they land and taxi in, and then the dispersal hut is full of flushed, excited pilots with tousled hair and red marks around their faces where helmets and oxygen masks have been, all talking and shouting at once, while a harassed intelligence officer tries to sort some sense out of six different types all telling him different things at the same time. Sometimes everyone is very sober and quiet, and you gather that Jack has bought it, or Bill had to force land, but luckily that doesn't happen very often. Finally the I.O. is satisfied that he's got the gen and leaves the somewhat calmer boys to tell you what happened, what the flak was like, and ask anxiously how the formation looked. Then everyone settles down to wait for the next show to come up. It all looks much more dramatic on paper than it really is — or maybe it's because I've seen it all so often that I'm rather blasé. Anyway, I hope you find it interesting and the censor doesn't cut this page out!

Must dash off to bed now darling — again. I have to be up early — even earlier tomorrow — 5:45 am, or some such ridiculous hour. Bonsoir.

> All my love dearest,
> Eric

P.S. Sorry, I've addressed the envelope upside down.

Here we go :—

Oh, I have slipped the surly bonds of Earth
And danced the skies on laughter-silvered wings;
Sunward I've climbed, and joined the tumbling mirth
Of sun-split clouds - and done a hundred things
You have not dreamed of - wheeled and soared and swung
High in the sunlit silence; hov'ring there,
I've chased the shouting wind along, and flung
My eager craft through footless halls of air.

Up, up the long, delirious, burning blue
I've topped the wind-swept heights with easy grace
Where never lark, or even eagle flew -
And, while with silent lifting mind I've trod
The high untrespassed sanctity of space,
Put out my hand and touched the face of God.

That is a complete answer to the question people who've never flown always ask me - "What's it like flying up there all alone?" I don't think I've ever seen it expressed so well before - flying is the hardest thing to put into words - but this chap has done it perfectly. Feel you'd like to fly? I'll take you up sometime.

CHAPTER TWELVE

Slipping the Surly Bonds of Earth

On April 12th 1945 Eric failed to return from a sortie and was listed as "Missing in Action." In the early afternoon he was flying his Hawker Typhoon Mark 1B aircraft east of Walle, Germany, on the hunt for targets. Going down to attack a train he met considerable flak. "Hutch" as he was popularly known by his 182 Squadron colleagues, continued the attack behind his leader, Squadron Leader John Derry, and was hit in the engine. Calling up Derry on his radio he was calmly heard to report that he couldn't last long and would try to make the Allied lines some 20 miles distant. His number two followed as an escort but, in trouble himself, was unable to follow "Hutch" to the ground. The last that Derry heard from the gallant flier was when he reported that it was unlikely he would make it back to his Enschede base and would have to force-land in enemy territory.

April 12, 1945
From the Air Ministry Operations Record Book:

A fair morning with threat of rain but only a few showers resulted. It was not long before we were operating, for at 12.10 Sdn/Ldr. Derry led 8 aircraft on an armed reconnaissance of the Rottenburg – Retham area. The Roundburg marshalling yard was inspected but no movement was seen. A locomotive and twenty trucks were attacked – the loco being damaged and one truck destroyed. A second loco and seven trucks were attacked, the loco being destroyed and two trucks damaged. The passengers were seen to scatter wildly in all directions. Some movement on the roads were seen and attacked, four Met being damaged and four destroyed. Flak posts in a village were also attacked with RP and cannon with considerable success. Flt/Lt. Hutchin had the misfortune to be hit by flak and was forced to crash land. No further news has been heard from him and he has been posted as missing.

The rest of the squadron returned to base at 13.40 At 16.15 F/O Jackson and seven others were scrambled to co-operate with Dalslock. Great confusion was caused through Scallywag calling up and giving a four figure map reference. The squadron was unable to locate the target owing to poor visibility and no assistance was received from Scallywag, only a considerable amount of distinctive criticism. All aircraft returned to base at 18.10 without making any attacks. During the whole day the adjutant was on the road from Helmond with "B" party, when they eventually arrived at Enschede they were greeted by the news that they were off to Rheine in the morning. We do sure get around.

Records held by the Air Ministry contain the following information:

On Thursday 12 April 1945 the aircraft of 182 Squadron were airborne at 12.10 in search of trains in the Rotenburg area. Flt. Lt. Hutchin was flying as Red 3 in Typhoon SW391. During an attack on a train a considerable amount of light flak was encountered and Flt. Lt. Hutchin called up to say that he had been hit by flak and was streaming glycol (coolant). He set out for a safer area accompanied by another aircraft from the Squadron. Flt .Lt. Hutchin's aircraft steadily lost height and he was reported as calling up to say that he was about to jettison his hood and make a crash landing. Nothing further was seen or heard from him.

CHAPTER THIRTEEN
The Family Waits

Eric's parents were notified by telegram on 14th April 1945 that Eric was missing in action. I remember Granny saying that she saw the "telegram boy" walking up the path and that she feared the worst. In those days it was not possible for the next of kin to be notified by a personal visit due to the large number of casualties the Royal Air Force had to deal with.

Text of telegram from Air Ministry (Casualty Branch) to Mr. P. Hutchin, 14th April 1945:

REGRET TO INFORM YOU THAT YOUR SON FLIGHT LIEUTENANT E.G.HUTCHIN (NO 150040) IS REPORTED MISSING AS THE RESULT OF AIR OPERATIONS ON 12 APRIL. ENQUIRIES ARE BEING MADE THROUGH THE INTERNATIONAL RED CROSS COMMITTEE. ANY FURTHER INFORMATION RECEIVED WILL BE COMMUNICATED TO YOU IMMEDIATELY. SHOULD NEWS OF HIM REACH YOU FROM ANY OTHER SOURCE PLEASE ADVISE THIS DEPARTMENT. MISS McKENZIE IS BEING INFORMED. LETTER FOLLOWS SHORTLY

Immediately following that telegram, Percy Hutchin, Eric's father, received a letter from Squadron Leader John Derry giving an account of what happened.

128376 Sqdn/Ldr Derry
182 Sqdn., R.A.F., B.L.A. (British Liberation Army)

14.4.45 (April 14th, 1945)

To Mr. P. Hutchin, 154 London Road, Morden, Surrey

Dear Sir,

I am afraid that I am not able to give you very much information about your son at the time of writing. However, I know that you must be very anxious and it is my practice to write immediately to next of kin, so I will give you the information I have at present. We were out on a hunt for targets near Bremen on 12th April at about 12:30 midday. Hutch, as he was always known on the squadron, was flying as my sub-section leader. We went down to attack a train and met considerable flak. Hutch, however, attacked behind me in spite of the opposition and was hit in the engine. He called me up quite calmly saying that his engine wouldn't last long and that he would try to reach our lines some twenty miles distant. His number two followed him as escort but was in trouble himself, so naturally couldn't follow Hutch down to the ground. The last time Hutch called me up he said he was unlikely to make the front and would force land. After that I heard nothing.

I naturally do not want to give you false hope but I myself have strong hopes for his safe return though I think he is almost certainly a prisoner. However, since we know nothing of what happened after his last call I do not wish to say too much. I hope you understand the position in spite of the lack of information and appreciate that I want you to know all that I know but not to draw any conclusions.

I would like to say that I am with you in your anxiety for Hutch's safety. He is one of my best pilots and one in whom I have the utmost confidence. His calmness in reporting his difficulties to me was a credit to the squadron and a fine example to others. Hutch is a personal friend of mine since I was in this squadron with him before becoming C.O. I will write as soon as I have any further information in the meantime will do all I can to find out more.

Yours sincerely, Squadron Leader Derry

The following letter of confirmation was sent to Eric's parents stating that Flt.Lt. Hutchin was missing as a result of air operations.

<u>Text of letter from Air Ministry (Casualty Branch)</u>
<u>to Mr P S Hutchin dated 21 April 1945.</u>

I am commanded by the Air Council to confirm the telegram in which you were notified that your son, Flight Lieutenant Eric Geoffrey Hutchin, Royal Air Force, is missing as the result of air operations on 12 April 1945.

The telegraphic report from your son's Unit states that the Typhoon aircraft in which he set out for an armed reconnaissance of the Rethem area, Germany, was hit by enemy anti-aircraft fire. The last known position of the aircraft was approximately five miles north east of Verden when your son called over his radio and stated that he was making a forced landing.

If your son is a prisoner of war he may possibly be able to communicate with you. Present conditions in Germany, however, largely preclude communication, and the International Red Cross Committee no longer expects to receive reports from the German authorities. Should any news of him be received, you will, of course be informed at once.

The Air Council desire me to express their sympathy with you in your anxiety.

Eric's parents then received the following telegram:.

REGRET TO INFORM YOU THAT YOUR SON, FLIGHT LIEUTENANT ERIC GEOFFREY HUTCHIN (150040) IS NOW REPORTED MISSING AND BELIEVED TO HAVE LOST HIS LIFE AS THE RESULT OF AIR OPERATIONS ON 12 APRIL. ANY FURTHER INFORMATION RE-CEIVED WILL BE COMMUNICATED TO YOU IMMEDI-ATELY. MISS McKENZIE IS BEING INFORMED. LETTER FOLLOWS SHORTLY.

In June the crash site of Eric's aircraft was located and the following letter came from the Air Ministry.

Text of letter dated 28 June 1945 from Air Ministry (Casualty Branch) to Mr P S Hutchin.

I am commanded by the Air Council to inform you that they have with great regret to confirm the telegram in which you were notified that your son, Flight Lieutenant Eric Geoffrey Hutchin, Royal Air Force, is now believed to have lost his life as the result of air operations on 12 April 1945.

Royal Air Force authorities on the continent have reported that the wreckage of the aircraft in which your son was flying has been found near Buchholz approximately 30 miles south east of Bremen and that they were informed that your son's body was buried by the Germans near the scene of the crash.

There is unhappily no reason to doubt the accuracy of this in-formation, and the necessary steps for the formal presumption, for official purposes, of your son's death will be taken shortly. A further letter on that subject will be addressed to you as soon as possible.

The Air Council desire me to express their profound sympathy with you in your bereavement.

In September 1945 a letter from the Air Ministry sent the official confirmation:

<u>Text of letter dated 19 September 1945 from the Air Ministry</u>
<u>(Directorate of Personal Services) to Mr P. S. Hutchin</u>

I am directed to refer to the letter from this Department of 28 June 1945, and to inform you that action has now been taken to presume, for official purposes, that your son, Flight Lieutenant E.G. Hutchin lost his life on 12 April 1945

In August 2012 while I was writing this book I contacted the Air Ministry and they sent me typed copies of the above correspondence along with a letter from the Air Ministry quoting their records as follows:

On Thursday 12th April 1945 the aircraft of 182 Squadron were airborne at 12.10 pm in search of trains in the Rottenburg area. Flt/Lt Hutchin was flying as Red 3 in Typhoon SW391. During an attack on a train a considerable amount of light flak was encountered and Flt/Lt Hutchin called up to say that he had been hit by flak and was streaming glycol (coolant). He set out for a safer area accompanied by another aircraft from the Squadron. Flt/Lt Hutchin's aircraft steadily lost height and he was reported as calling up to say he was about to jettison his hood and make a crash landing. Nothing further was seen or heard from him.

At the end of June 1945 151 Repair and Salvage Unit found the wreckage of Flt/Lt Hutchin's Typhoon near Bucholz at map reference X236903. They also reported that Flt/Lt Hutchin had been buried about 50 yards from his aircraft.

<u>Text of letter dated 3 October 1945 from Air Ministry</u>
<u>to Mr P.S. Hutchin</u>

I have with great regret, to refer again to the loss of your dear son. You would wish to know that the attached photograph of his resting place was taken by a member of the Royal Electrical and Mechanical Engineers, at present serving in Germany.

Eric's kin took some comfort in knowing that in death Eric's body was treated with respect and thanks to this photograph from the R.E.M.E. they knew that his body was recovered from the wreckage of his aircraft by person or persons unknown and placed in a temporary grave with a wooden cross.

In October 1945 Eric's mother received the following letter from Frances. Eric had left instructions with his squadron for Frances to be notified should anything happen to him.

Pomona College

October 1, 1945

Dear Mrs. Hutchin,

I received your letter a short time ago and felt very much ashamed of myself for not having written before, but I just didn't know quite what to say in a letter to you. Yes, I was notified by the Royal Air Force Delegation in Washington D.C. and later received a short letter from Eric's Squadron Leader. It didn't give much detail but was very sweet and praised Eric very highly both as a companion and a pilot.

I can only add to what he said. As you undoubtedly know, I was a hostess at the British War Relief Society in Phoenix and met Eric through a girl friend at one of the social functions given by that organization. I think we probably liked each other, particularly at first, because we liked to dance together. But later as I began to see more of him and his friend, Ian Briscoe as well, I found that I liked everything I saw about them both. They were very much alike and it's no wonder that they got on so well together. Really Mrs. Hutchin, it is a wonderful tribute to you as his mother to have had such a fine boy as Eric.

Of all the hundreds of boys that I met through the British Center in the two years that I was associated with it, there were extremely few who could hold a candle to Eric as far as character was concerned — and of course none that I was more fond of. He didn't come to my home until a very short time before he left but in that time my mother and father became almost as fond of him as I was. Many of the boys that my friends and I have known have been killed in this terrible war which is at last mercifully over, but none has struck at my heart quite as forcibly as the news of Eric.

Please accept my heartfelt sympathy, Mrs. Hutchin, and I do pray that your other two sons are safe and will be home to stay very soon.

Very sincerely, Frances

At the cessation of the hostilities Eric's remains were disinterred by the Commonwealth Graves Commission and formal identification confirmation took place before Eric was finally laid to rest in the British Military Cemetery at Soltau, Germany.

Moved from Bucholz to Soltau.
This is before the granite headstones were installed.

BUCKINGHAM PALACE

The Queen and I offer you our heartfelt sympathy in your great sorrow.

We pray that your country's gratitude for a life so nobly given in its service may bring you some measure of consolation.

George R.I.

P. S. Hutchin, Esq.

Correspondence on the subject
of this letter should be
addressed to
THE UNDER-SECRETARY
OF STATE,
AIR MINISTRY....................
and should quote the reference
..............P.431704/45/S.14.Cas.C.5.

Your Ref. ....

AIR MINISTRY,
LONDON, W.C.2.
2, Seville Street,
London, S.W.1.

26 February, 1948.

Sir,

I am directed to inform you that your son's grave has
now been removed from Bucholz to the British cemetery at
Soltau (Becklingen) seven miles south south east of Soltau,
Germany.

It is the policy of the Graves Registration Service to
transfer all the graves of British personnel who lost their
lives in Germany into British Military Cemeteries in that
country, where they will be maintained, in perpetuity, by
the Imperial War Graves Commission.

When the work on the Cemetery has been completed you
will be notified of the registered Plot, Row and Grave number.

I am, Sir,
Your obedient Servant,

Staynton.

P.S. Hutchin, Esq.,
154, London Road,
Morden,
Surrey.

CS

Tel. No. Sloane 3467

ABBEY 3411, Ext...............

P.431704/S.14.Cas.C.7

AIR MINISTRY,

~~WHITEHALL~~,

~~LONDON, S.W.1.~~

2, Seville Street,
Knightsbridge,
London, S.W.1.

/2 August, 1948

Dear Mr. Hutchin,

     With reference to the letter from this Department of 22nd February last, the Royal Air Force Missing Research and Enquiry Service have now reported that your son's grave has been registered as No. 1B, Row B, Plot XIX, in Soltau (Becklingen) British Military Cemetery.

     I do sincerely hope the knowledge that his last resting place will always be reverently tended by the Imperial War Graves Commission may be of some slight comfort to you.

Yours sincerely,

[signature]

P.S. Hutchin, Esq.,
154 London Road,
Morden,
Surrey.

CHAPTER FOURTEEN
Soltau

In 1994, along with my brother Paul, I travelled to Germany to visit Eric's grave. We were the first members of the family to do so. Although my grandparents had been offered that option by the War Commission, they chose not to go. My grandmother, coincidentally also named Frances, never recovered from the loss of her youngest son and could not bear the thought of making that journey.

Upon arrival at Becklingen Cemetary in Soltau, Paul and I found the grave listed in the cemetery register and spent time paying our respects to our brave uncle and hero who lost his life fighting for our freedom. We were driven to Soltau by two dear German friends from Hamburg, Ulli Paasch and Peter Zeiger, who, to this very day, travel to the grave on April 12th of each year to lay flowers on Eric's grave on behalf of the family. The cemetery is built on a hillside overlooking the site where Field Marshall Montgomery accepted surrender from Admiral Dönitz on May 4th 1945. The cemetery is the final resting place for 2,374 military personnel from the British Commonwealth, most of whom lost their lives during the last two months of the war. The site is maintained in perpetuity by the Imperial War Graves Commission.

TOP: The cemetery register is in this archway at the entrance to Becklingen Cemetery.

MIDDLE: Walking in to the cemetery. "Their name liveth for evermore."

BOTTOM: The monument overlooking the cemetery

The author and her brother Paul Hutchin.

Rest in Peace, our beloved Eric

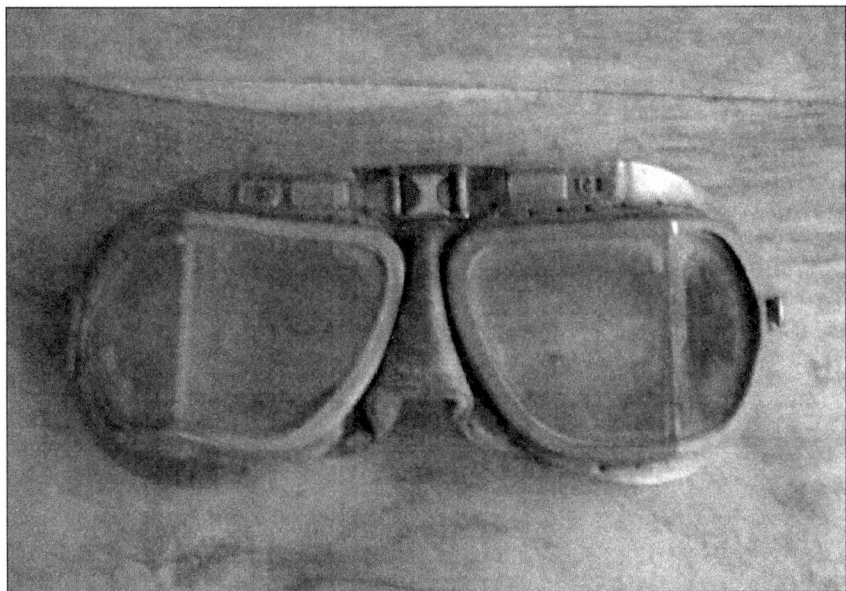

Eric's medals, received by his parents after the war.

FROM LEFT TO RIGHT: 1939-1945 Star Battle of Britain,
1939-1945 War Medal, and Air Crew Europe Star

The Under-Secretary of State for
Air presents his compliments and
by Command of the Air Council
has the honour to transmit the
enclosed Awards granted for service
in the war of 1939-45.
The Council share your sorrow that

Flight Lieutenant E. G. Hutchin

in respect of whose service these
Awards are granted did not
live to receive them.

Note received in the box with Eric's medals.

CHAPTER FIFTEEN
My Uncle... My Hero

For as long as I can remember Frances Mackenzie was a name and address in my grandparents address book; an enigma, a romantic fantasy to this little girl who grew up playing in the ruins of the bombed buildings of south London. Upon asking my grandparents about Frances they would tell me "oh, that was the girl Uncle Eric fell in love with during the war." My Uncle Eric was their youngest son, a Royal Air Force fighter pilot. He and many other R.A.F. pilots were trained at Falcon Field in Mesa, Arizona. I associated his name with those famous words of Winston Churchill: "Never in the field of human conflict was so much owed by so many to so few." I applied those words, dedicated to the pilots who participated in the Battle of Britain, to all young men of the Royal Air Force.

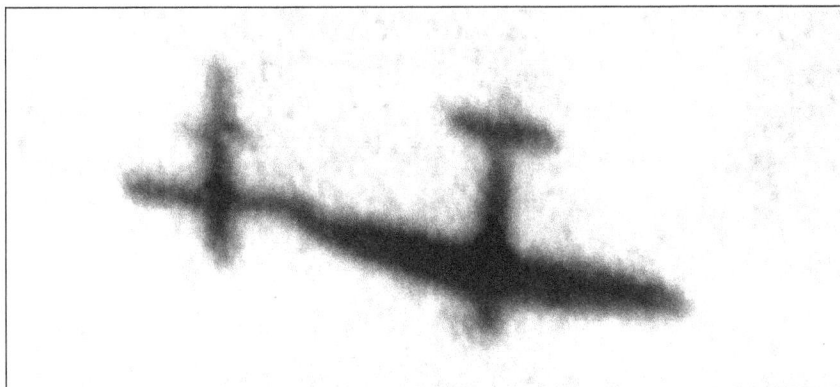

Seen in silhouette, a Royal Air Force Supermarine Spitfire (on the right) manoeuvres alongside a German V-1 flying bomb in an attempt to tip its wing and topple its gyros, disrupting the missile's automatic pilot and deflecting it from its target and causing it to crash. *Picture courtesy Wikipedia.*

To me, my uncle, Flight Lieutenant Eric Hutchin, was one of those "few," a daring young Royal Air Force pilot whose courage kept the Nazis from the shores of England. When Hitler was bombarding England with V-1 rockets (known as "Doodlebugs") I remember being told that Eric and his squadron would fly their Spitfires out over the English Channel and with great daring and precision they would flip the rockets around with the tips of their aircraft wings and "send them back to Germany."

For the civilians in England these were dark and terrible days. Fresh food was virtually non-existent, petrol was on ration and then was only allocated for special services. All houses had blackout curtains so that not even a small chink of light shone through to give the German planes any clue as to what was below. Everyone did their part. Women worked in munitions factories and toiled in the fields; elderly men not able to fight worked as Air Raid Wardens, riding bicycles through the streets ringing a hand bell to warn people of impending air strikes and bombing raids. People would scurry to the air raid shelters or down into the Un-

St Paul's Cathedral, December 1941. *Source Wikipedia.*

derground train stations not knowing when they might emerge again. Oftentimes they would come out of the shelters to utter devastation.

Somehow the "stiff upper lip" attributed to the English got them through the war. Their sense of humour was amazing and their favourite saying was "Don't panic and carry on regardless"! I was the eldest of seven children and we grew up listening to war stories around the Sunday dinner table; we would ask to hear the same stories time and time again.

All these thoughts flooded my mind in November 1993 as I stepped out of the car in Phoenix, Arizona and walked up to the door of Frances McKenzie's house whose address was imprinted in my mind from my grandparents' address book. No-one was home but I felt the presence of my uncle around me. It wasn't until a year later, when my father came over to America for a visit, that I decided to write a letter to the resident family at that address, asking them if they had any knowledge of the McKenzie family. About three days after I posted the letter I received a phone call from a gentleman who told me that he had bought the house from the McKenzies 25 years earlier, and was still in touch with the family. Soon after, Claude McKenzie called to say that he would pass my contact information on to his sister, Frances.

About two weeks later I answered the phone and heard a soft voice with an American accent say, "Hello, this is Frances McKenzie." I could hardly talk. Tears filled my eyes and I was at a loss for words. I managed to say that I was the niece of Eric Hutchin and that I lived in Tucson.

"Do you remember Eric?" I asked.

"Yes. He used to write me the most beautiful letters."

When I asked her if she still had the letters she reminded me it had been more than 50 years ago and she had been married for a long time and had grown children.

I told her that my father was here to visit from England and asked if she would mind very much if we came to Phoenix to meet her. She graciously agreed, and so a week later we drove up to Phoenix and met the enigma who was Frances McKenzie.

As I sat drinking an iced tea, she walked over and put a handful of air mail letters on my lap. Daddy and I locked eyes.

"I didn't think I had these," she said, "but I found them and would like you to have them."

I looked at them, tears rolled down my cheeks and onto the precious memories in my hand. I wanted to ask her so many questions, but here she was, over 70 years old with her husband of 50 years at her side, so we really just made small talk until it was time to go back to Tucson.

Over the next few weeks Daddy and I sat trying to read the letters but barely got through more than a couple of pages at a time before Daddy would say "We had better go and make a cup of tea." It was during that time that I decided to write this book. The letters were poignant at times and so insightful that I wanted to share them. I have always been so thankful to Frances for saving these letters and giving me the opportunity to learn so much about the man I had loved and admired for my entire life.

CHAPTER SIXTEEN

Memories and Memorials

Some of the many tributes paid to these brave young airmen who never lived to realise their dreams.

A Beautiful Tribute

This poem was written by an unknown Dutch lady in the summer of 1945. It speaks eloquently of these brave and wonderful young pilots.

When I look at the sky over Holland at night
The blue dome and the stars are all tranquil and bright
It is peaceful and still, not a sound to be heard
But the rustling of leaves and the cry of a bird.

Not a bomber, no fighters on high any more
And no crisscrossing searchlights as in days of war.
All is peaceful and still for the enemy has gone
And the battle for freedom was finally won.

When we sat in the path of the bombers at night
We felt anxious but glad; for their every flight
Did bring nearer the day when the Nazis would flee,
When the war would be over and we would be free.

We all prayed with great fervor and often cried out
"Oh Lord keep them safe, let them quickly dive out
Of the crossroads of searchlights high up in the sky
And oh please save their lives, oh God don't let them die."

The young children all prayed "send us so many planes
that the sparrows can't fly and must walk in the lanes";
and the parents prayed "please let them soon free us all
from the Teutons' mad fury that holds us in thrall."

Though so many were lost in the terrible fight
While we watched and prayed anxiously many a night,
Their endeavours and courage have not been in vain:
For by them and their comrades the Nazis were slain.

When I looked at the sky over Holland last night
The blue dome and the stars were all tranquil and bright.
There is peace, no more sirens, I heard a bird call.
OH WE THANK YOU, BRAVE AIRMEN, MAY GOD BLESS YOU
ALL.

From We Flew the Rocket Firing Typhoon

The memorial at Noyers Bocage

In 1990, thanks to the efforts of Mr. Jaques Brehin, President of the Association de Ailes pour le Souvenir des Ailes de la Victoire se Normandie, a memorial was raised for the 150 Typhoon pilots who were killed in action during the Battle of Normandy (June 1944). The Memorial can be found on a grass field along the N175 road between Caen and Villers Bocage.

Photograph and information courtesy the Royal Netherlands Air Force, History Unit. From We Flew the Rocket Firing Typhoon.

The Last Typhoon

This particular aircraft was originally sent to the United States in March 1944 for fighter comparison and evaluation trials. In the late 1940s General Henry "Hap" Arnold, Chief of Staff of the US Army Air Force, collected together 60 WWII aircraft from all over the world and had them stored in an unused Douglas Aircraft Company factory in Chicago, Illinois.

My father (Eric's brother Ernie) in 2008, in front of the MN235, the only remaining HawkerTyphoon. Royal Air Force Museum, Hendon, North London.

In April 1967 the Royal Air Force Museum in Hendon requested that the Typhoon be shipped back to England. The following year the Smithsonian presented the Typhoon to the Royal Air Force Museum in exchange for a Hawker Hurricane. Over the years a great deal of restoration work was completed by a dedicated team of volunteers. It was moved to Hendon in 1972 for the museum opening and has been displayed ever since in an area known as the "The Fighter Hall." Invasion stripes were applied to the wings and fuselage and the MN235 is the sole surviving complete Typhoon.

Courtesy www.rafmuseum.org.uk

Falcon Field Airport and Commemorative Air Force, Arizona Wing, Aviation Museum

Falcon Field is still an operational and active airport owned and by the City of Mesa. Adjoining Falcon Field is the Commemorative Air Force Arizona Wing Aviation Museum. The museum features planes from World War I and World War II as well as more modern jet fighters. Most of the planes are originals and some are replicas but all of them are flyable. The museum is often visited by veterans who like to reminisce about these planes.

The museum is the home and headquarters of the Commemorative Air Force, Arizona Wing and is dedicated to preserving the memory and the history of those that have given so much, and asked for so little in return. They are continually compiling stories from veterans and their families of both U.S. and British Veterans to serve as living history for years to come.

On Veterans Day weekend every year the Wing conducts a memorial service to honour young Royal Air Force Cadets who lost their lives during training at Falcon Field.

www.azcaf.org

Falcon Field Park/Mesa

Just a stone's throw from the airfield is Falcon Field Park, located at 4800 E. Falcon Field Drive. The original stone fireplace from the cadets' lounge at the Falcon Field barracks was saved and relocated to the park.

Photographs courtesy Daryl Mallett.

Royal Air Force Cadet Memorial

On Veterans Day in November of each year a memorial service is held at the Mesa Cemetery to honour the 23 Royal Air Force Cadets who died while training at Falcon Field. We also remember the 1,500

ABOVE: Wreaths placed at the cemetery by visiting dignitaries

RIGHT: In loving memory ... A small corner of Arizona that is forever England

cadets who trained there and went on to serve in World War II. Fewer and fewer surviving cadets attend the ceremony each year. A "Dinner With Legends" is held the evening before. Traditional Scottish bagpipers play at the service which culminates with a treetop flyover of vintage WWII aircraft.

This is me with Ken Beeby at Falcon Field, November 15th, 2011. Ken was at Falcon Field at the same time as my Uncle Eric, and received his wings there. Upon his return to England he was made a flight instructor and amongst his students were pilots from Australia and New Zealand who were given navigational courses before they were trained for European operations. He is involved with the Falcon Field Association and now makes his home in Tempe, Arizona, quite close to Falcon Field, where he attends the memorial ceremony in November each year. We are close and I treasure our friendship.

On Veterans Day in England people wear a red poppy in honour of those who lost their lives in the World Wars.

Commemorative Air Force, Arizona Wing, Aviation Museum

The Commemorative Air Force (CAF) was founded to acquire, restore and preserve in flying condition a complete collection of combat aircraft which were flown by all military services of the United States, and selected aircraft of other nations, for the education and enjoyment of present and future generations of Americans.

More than just a collection of airworthy warplanes from the past, the CAF's fleet of historic aircraft, known as the CAF Ghost Squadron, recreate, remind and reinforce the lessons learned from the defining moments in American military aviation history.

The CAF Arizona Wing is one of approximately 75 units that comprise the totality of the CAF and is the largest unit in the organization. The museum is located in the southwest corner of Falcon Field in Mesa, Arizona and is an educational and commemorative non-profit organization dedicated to preserving the history of those that have given so much, and asked for so little in return. The Arizona Wing is the official repository of the archives of the R.A.F. Falcon Field Association, retaining the memorabilia of those R.A.F. cadets that trained at #4 British Flying Training School (Falcon Field) during World War II.

On Veterans Day weekend the Wing conducts an annual memorial service for the 23 young British aviators who died in accidents while in training in Mesa. They are continually compiling stories from veterans and their families of their military experiences and from the home front. These experiences will be retained for future generations as living history.

Courtesy Larry A. Turner, Wing Leader
Commemorative Air Force, Arizona Wing
www.azcaf.org

Mesa - Falcon Field Airport

Groundbreaking ceremonies were conducted on the same day - July 16, 1941 - for both Falcon Field and Williams Field that served as World War II pilot training bases and now serve Mesa and the East Valley in different capacities. Arizona's dry climate and open spaces made it an ideal choice for training air troops.

Mesa - Falcon Field Airport

Falcon Field opened in September 1941 as a military airport to train British Royal Air Force and U.S. Army Air Force pilots. The first training flight was an American-made Boeing PT-17 "Stearman" biplane. In 1948 the federal government deeded the property to the City of Mesa as a municipal airport. The City contracted daily operations through a private operator until 1968, when it assumed this responsibility. Falcon Field includes a total of 784 acres owned by the City. The primary one-square-mile airport campus is located between Greenfield, Higley, McDowell and McKellips roads in northeast Mesa.

Today, Falcon Field is a general aviation (GA) reliever airport that serves as an alternative for civilian and military aviation uses such as business, recreation, and fixed-wing and helicopter flight training so that

Present day Falcon Field

Phoenix Sky Harbor International Airport and Phoenix-Mesa Gateway Airport (formerly Williams Field, located in southeast Mesa near the Loop 202 Freeway and Power Road) can focus on international and domestic commercial airline services.

Air space around Falcon Field is managed by the Federal Aviation Administration (FAA). In 2011 there were more than 229,000 total aircraft operations (take-offs and landings) at the airport.

www.falconfieldairport.com

ABOUT THE AUTHOR

Catherine Hutchin was born in November 1943 during an air raid. Growing up in post-war London, the eldest of seven children born to an English father and an Irish mother, she was always acutely aware of the sacrifices made by the young men of the Royal Air Force. An appreciation of their bravery is something she has carried with her throughout her life.

In 1967 Catherine flew to Los Angeles on what her father referred to as a "Pan Am four-prop job!" There she opened Transatlantic Management to pursue a career managing and promoting rock'n'roll bands, including a highly talented teenage Van Halen. After a refreshing interlude living in a teepee in northeast Oregon raising sheep, cattle, pigs and chickens, in 1980 she relocated to Tucson, Arizona, lured by the beauty of the Sonoran Desert. Known to her friends as EC, for English Cathy, she reopened Transatlantic Management, promoted local bands and opened a teenage night club, The Pink Cadillac, a place that is still fondly remembered by locals approaching their 40s. At the annual South By Southwest Music and Media Conference in Austin, she represented many Tucson-based musicians as well as others from various cities around America. In 1987 Catherine met Greg Harris at a U2 concert. They fell in love and have been together ever since, marrying in 1997 on the ten-year anniversary of the night they met. EC is a romantic.

Transatlantic Management remained active until 2004, when Catherine retired from the music business. She is now on the board of several non-profit corporations including the Celtic Academy of Tucson, the St. Patrick's Day Parade and Festival, and the Tucson Irish Heritage Foundation.

REFERENCES & RESOURCES

Jim Dawson. *The RAF in Arizona: Falcon Field — 1941–1945.* Stenger-Scott Publishing, 2002.

Daryl F. Mallett. *Images of America: Falcon Field.* Arcadia Publishing, 2009.

Dr. John Rickard. "Typhoon 1B statistics and squadron locations", www.historyofwar.org.

Larry J. Simmons. *Falcon Field: Life at Arizona's Falcon Field During WWII.* Larry J. Simmons, 2004.

Andrew Simpson, Curator, Department of Aircraft and Exhibitors, Royal Air Force Museum, Hendon, England. "The Hawker Typhoon's place in history". www.rafmuseum.org

Wing Leader Larry A. Turner. Commemorative Air Force, Arizona Wing, Aviation Museum, Mesa, Arizona. www.azcaf.org

Dr. P.E. van Loo, ed. *We Flew the Rocket Firing Typhoon: World War II Memories of 124 Wing RAF Pilots and Supporting Staff.* Royal Netherlands Air Force, History Unit, The Hague, 1998.

David A. Walker. "Falcon: Where a Hollywood Contact Helped Win a War." AOPA April 1984.

_____. British Flying Training School Museum, Terrell, Texas. www.bftsmuseum.org.

_____. "English Air Men Coming." Mesa Journal, Aug. 1, 1941.

_____. " Epilogue." 1942. www.ww2aircraft.net.

_____. "Mesa — Falcon Field Airport." www.falconfieldairport.com.

_____. Ministry of Defence, Middlesex, England.

www.AircrewRemembranceSociety.com.

CPSIA information can be obtained
at www.ICGtesting.com
Printed in the USA
LVHW050822060921
697056LV00006B/66